ON WRITING EDUCATIONAL ETHNOGRAPHIES:
THE ART OF COLLUSION

ON WRITING EDUCATIONAL ETHNOGRAPHIES:
THE ART OF COLLUSION

ON WRITING EDUCATIONAL ETHNOGRAPHIES:
THE ART OF COLLUSION

Jean Conteh, Eve Gregory, Chris Kearney,
Aura Mor-Sommerfeld

Trentham Books

Stoke on Trent, UK and Sterling, USA

Trentham Books Limited
Westview House   22883 Quicksilver Drive
734 London Road   Sterling
Oakhill   VA 20166-2012
Stoke on Trent   USA
Staffordshire
England ST4 5NP

© 2005 Jean Conteh, Eve Gregory, Chris Kearney, Aura Mor-Sommerfeld

First published 2005

British Library Cataloguing-in-Publication Data
A catalogue record for this book is available from the British Library

ISBN-13: 978-1-85856-341-1
ISBN-10: 1-85856-341-0

Designed and typeset by Trentham Print Design Ltd, Chester and printed in Great Britain by Bemrose Shafron (Printers) Ltd, Chester.

CONTENTS

All four authors have shared equally in the
construction of this book.

Eve would like to dedicate this book to her mother, Elsie.

Introduction:
Tracing the steps
Eve Gregory

I am just a boy
with a lot of dreams
but what's the point
I won't get nowhere
I'm just ordinary
nothing special just
...ordinary
got no chance in this
world unless you're
...clever
which I'm not.

(Thirteen-year-old boy in *Stepney Words*, 1973)

What typifies ethnography in education as a research approach? Much of what we need to know is crystallised in the words of the thirteen-year-old cited above: ethnography in education speaks up for those who are 'just ordinary'. By making visible the lives of people whose stories are not often told, it gives a voice to all of us who are 'nothing special'. It delves into possible reasons why both this particular boy and similar boys generally 'won't get nowhere', who determines why he has 'got no chance in this world unless he is clever' and probes into why he is so sure that he is not. Ultimately, by digging out assumptions, beliefs and practices taking place between 'just plain folks', it hopes to push all of us involved into asking 'Why must things be the way they are?' and, armed with this knowledge, changing our lives for the better. In this chapter, I begin to trace the Why? What? and How? of ethnography in education, concentrating particularly on the Why? and the What? and inviting Jean, Chris and Aura to illustrate the How? of the task in the chapters that follow. Throughout the chapter, I argue that all ethnographic studies start by having an important story to be told, a story that lies deep within the soul.

Beginnings: why choose ethnography?

Derelict Dock

Silence moves through the dock,
No one around but an old dog.
Cranes all rusty, dirty and old,
Engines broken down, long ago.
The river moves quietly,
Not a boat to be seen.
No people anywhere near now,
Drinking beer, near the canal.

Tracey Crane, 12 in *Classrooms of Resistance* (1975)

The beginnings of an ethnographic study are often rooted in anger, even fury, and, as such, are partisan. A chance encounter with a book, a classroom incident, a teacher, child or parent's remark will often be enough to spark a deep-seated anger or an unanswered question from deep in our own past, which initiates the study. Margaret Meek has often referred to this eloquently as 'the paradigmatic moment' that both symbolises and illustrates the central or big question of the study, a moment we keep returning to throughout the work and which we never forget.

My own way into ethnography was one such case. I became angry after reading a book written by three well-recognised sociologists during the 1970s, called *Depriving the Deprived* (Tunley, Travers and Pratt, 1979) which was generally acclaimed by academics as an insightful and telling study. The book was about people in London's East End; the area in which my own extended East End family had been born, schooled and, during the 1970s when the book was published, still worked and lived. In the sections following, I shall reveal how, although academically rigorous, the study unintentionally betrayed the communities it described. For it shows clearly how statistics can be used to provide 'evidence' for what local people know to be a nonsense. But this is jumping the gun. Let me tell the story properly.

The case made: statistics speak

The study began with two interlocking questions: How does one Education Authority – the London Borough of Newham – distribute its resources? Whilst recognising that there are no really privileged areas in the Borough in the traditionally accepted sense, is it distributing to areas that are most in need or is it privileging the privileged by devoting more resources to the less needy parts of the Borough?

To the authors, the questions were simple enough to answer: two very different areas of the Borough were chosen: the south of the Borough close to the Docks and previously known as West Ham and the north of the Borough close to Wanstead and Epping Forest and previously known as East Ham, and the areas were compared according to different indices of poverty. Indices chosen were standard and included unemployment, overcrowding, the absence of a bathroom or how many were sharing, whether or not English was spoken at home and eligibility for free school dinners. These were then matched against resources allocated to schools in the areas by the Education Authority. After measuring the comparative advantage or disadvantage of the two areas according to the chosen indices, the authors were able to claim that families in West Ham, the Dock area, were, comparatively speaking, more privileged than those living in East Ham, yet policies of the Education Authority had led to a higher funding of the west than the east, hence depriving the deprived. A clear-cut case, you might think.

Just plain folks: a different kind of knowledge

However, the matter was not that simple. Although the facts and figures seemed neatly to provide evidence to prove a certain case, the results of the study seemed quite extraordinary to those familiar with the area and its history, those known as 'just plain folks' or JPFs as they are sometimes called. Even teachers who travelled across

London to teach in the schools and were not familiar with the history of the area felt that the findings of the researchers were ridiculous. Everybody knew that the area of West Ham was less desirable than East Ham; those living in the high-rise Council flats to be pitied by those in larger houses with gardens in the east. Teachers, indeed, often referred to the Docklands children in West Ham as suffering from a 'deep poverty' transcending that of material goods in comparison with their more 'enlightened' peers often from Asian backgrounds in the east. So what had gone wrong? The just plain folks story ran quite differently to the proof offered by the University researchers since, unlike these, they either knew the history of the two areas and could explain why their populations were so different, or they used their eyes, ears and experience of teaching children in the area as well as conversing with their parents and families. The alternative story ran as follows.

A tale of two communities: West and East Ham

During the nineteenth century, the area around the Docks in West Ham, then the largest in the world, had undergone enormous industrialisation. Industries such as Silvers, the sugar factory which gave its name to Silvertown, the area next to the Docks, relied on cargo coming up the river from Britain's numerous colonies. The Docks needed massive casual labour for loading and unloading ships as and when they arrived. Their growth coincided with an increase in poverty in rural areas, partly due to the effects of the industrial revolution leading to the centralisation of cottage industries into larger factories. Increasing unemployment outside the capital coupled with expansion of trade in London meant that the East End had become a magnet for thousands coming from the countryside and desperate for work.[1]

Although the area directly around the Docks was not promising for building since it was originally marshland, the acute need for housing for workers meant that, bit by bit, land was drained and cheap accommodation built. Builders set up in business as quickly as they disappeared, sometimes leaving houses in a half-finished state until their finances improved. Those renting – and it was almost unknown to buy – lived in damp and insanitary conditions until main drainage was installed towards the end of the nineteenth century.

The Docks needed a steady supply of casual labour. Workers were exploited; foremen picked out those looking fittest and strongest on a daily basis, sending the rest home to depend upon wives forced to earn a pittance through sack or match-box making. Men chosen to work were given a 'ticket', an expression that continued to be used to identify the more elite group of permanent registered dockers until the time that the Docks closed.

Later, in the twentieth century, the General Strike of 1926 made matters worse. Men and women alike were forced back into work for less than they had earned before they came out on strike. The depression of the 1930s hit those working in the Docks hard, leading to many young men signing up.[2] Eventually, the greater problem of World War Two was to extend enlistment. Many men exchanged a life in the Docks for one in the Royal Navy or other armed forces, and not all returned. Those who did survive were frantic for news of their families. West Ham, and particularly the area around the Docks, was the precise target for Hitler's bombs. One Primary school suffered a direct bomb hit when it was full of families seeking shelter. Rumour was passed down across generations that it was West Ham Council's fault which had mistakenly sent the bus intended to take them to safety to the wrong school.

The bombed school was rebuilt during the 1950s, the land surrounding it untouched amidst high weeds since it had been consecrated. Most of the small terraced housing had either been destroyed or was unsafe. 'Best job the Jerries ever done' said many, remembering how primitive the houses had been. Little did they know that worse was still to come. Blocks of flats were erected, their height, starkness and bright, uniformly-coloured doors shocking to most. 'Ought to make the architects live in them' was the comment of many residents. It was lucky for them that they did not. One night in 1968, the first of the three blocks, a 23 storey skyscraper called Ronan Point in Clever Road, Canning Town was ripped apart by a gas explosion, killing five people. At the same time, the Docks were in trouble, unable to compete internationally with large container docks outside London and abroad and crippled by strikes. Eventually, and due partly to strikes at the end of the 1960s, the Newham docks closed completely, leaving a huge and painful gap in the lives of those who had depended upon them. Many ex-dockers took up casual labour such as mini-cabbing or left their wives to find work.

Such was the history of the community termed 'advantaged' in *Depriving the Deprived*. During the 1980s, some families had experienced both war losses and relatives caught in the Ronan Point disaster. Measured against the indices chosen by the academics, however, these families would have figured reasonably well. As Council tenants, they did not live in overcrowded conditions, all had bathrooms, registered unemployment was low and all spoke English as a first language.

Over in East Ham, the so-called underprivileged Borough by the researchers, things ran rather differently. During the mid-nineteenth century the main railway line from Essex to Liverpool Street in central London was built, opening up fast transport straight into the City of London, then, as now, seat of enormous wealth and offering a large number of white-collar jobs to service this. Houses sprang up along and around the line leading east from Stratford. It was indeed a desirable area, providing easy access to the golden square mile of the City and yet on the borders of the ancient Epping Forest. Even the names of different wards symbolised desirability. In contrast with Canning Town and Silvertown in West Ham, Forest Gate and Manor Park provided homes for bankers, doctors, civil servants and teachers. Many of the large detached houses in Forest Gate were built with small servants' quarters.

Until World War Two the area was solidly middle class, with parts being distinctly upper middle class in character. After the Second World War, however, the area fell rapidly out of fashion. Partly, the houses were too large for smaller families; partly, the area was becoming squeezed between the poorer East End closer to the City and new developments of Council estates for working class folk further east in Dagenham and Barking. Fords had opened huge works in Dagenham. During the 1950s and 1960s, most of the middle class inhabitants shifted further out of London to Essex or to more fashionable areas in central or west London. At the same time, a large influx of immigrants, mainly from the Caribbean, needed accommodation. The large houses were bought by unscrupulous landlords, turned into flats and let out privately to families, who often had to live in overcrowded conditions, lacking or sharing bathrooms. Families from the Caribbean were joined during the 1970s by families from India and Pakistan. Needless to say, by the criteria used in *Depriving the Deprived*, the area did indeed figure high in terms of poverty. Many families living in privately rented accommodation were in overcrowded conditions and sharing bathrooms. Registered unemployment and, consequently, numbers qualifying for free school dinners were high, as was the percentage of children learning English as a second language.

However, teachers and older established residents of the area knew circumstances to be different. Older residents still gave the leafy area an established feel. Teachers realised that there was a deeper type of optimism, a trust in education as a means to success that did not exist in the indigenous community of West Ham.

The crowning irony astonishing just plain folks was to hear that schools in West Ham *were* receiving more money than those in the east since, for just plain folks, that did not appear to be the case. Why *did* schools over in East Ham appear more generously staffed? Why was equipment newer and more freely distributed? The answer, again, needed ferreting out. Might it have been due to money coming from elsewhere, outside the LEA? Indeed, schools in East Ham during the 1970s were pleased to be well supplied by English as a Second Language teachers (Section 11 teachers), 75 per cent of whose salaries and equipment were met by funds from central government if a school went above a certain percentage of children from the New Commonwealth. Precisely these funds were not accounted for in the academic study! Such funding was highly important and certainly contributed to the considerable achievements of children who had only recently entered Britain speaking no English at all. When asked, most teachers would have felt that the West Ham indigenous English community was cut short in funding and desperately needed more resources. If they had heard, contrary to belief, that funds were being directed to the Docklands families, many would have agreed that, for once, a correct decision had been made by Newham Council.

Such was the story of *Depriving the Deprived*, the academics and the just plain folks.

Putting the self into the story

Why should this particular case-study have filled me with an anger that has led to twenty years of ethnographic research based on the home learning of children living in this area and in the adjacent Borough of Tower Hamlets? As an advisory teacher working during the 1980s in both East and West Ham, I suddenly realised that a different story from that of the academics needed to be told and that I was in a position to tell it. In the widest sense, *Depriving the Deprived* concerned my own family. Family stories permeated my interpretation of the text.[3]

All my grandparents had moved as children from the countryside to West Ham. One grandfather had become a milkman, delivering in the leafy streets of East Ham and my father recounted how, as a boy helping him before school, he had found a gold watch lying on the pavement. In contrast to families in his delivery round, my father had been beaten for wearing dirty shoes after running across the Borough to his school in West Ham and arriving late. Another grandfather had worked in the Gas Works in West Ham and died early of bronchitis when no-one could afford the 2/6d (about 12 new pence) to call out the doctor.

My parents' early work experiences in West Ham also permeated my interpretation of the text. The smell of molasses from the sugar refinery must have drifted through the Blackwall Tunnel from the south side of the river when my father pedalled his way amidst horse-drawn buses and lorries as a fourteen year old who had just left school. My mother also worked in the local factory in West Ham. As a fourteen-year-old, her wages dropped from 12/6d. (62p) to 10/- (50p) per week after the 1926 strike and her hours stayed rigidly at 48. Later, my uncle spent his whole working life as a docker without the coveted 'ticket' and my father told stories of the horror of nights during the blitz in Canning Town during World War Two. He had tried to help young children wandering aimlessly in the streets the night their parents had been killed in the bomb on the school.

As a teacher during the 1970s in East Ham, I enjoyed and was proud of the success of children who had entered my school unable to speak English. As an advisory teacher during the 1980s in West Ham, I shared the pain of eleven year olds unable to read and of their parents, supposedly unable to help them. I listened with horror to their teachers referring to the 'deep poverty' and 'lack of culture' they were supposed to suffer. Later, as a teacher educator in the neighbouring Borough of Tower Hamlets, I listened to a similar story about Bangladeshi British families. A lack of English literacy or, indeed, any literacy at all, were held to account for children's early literacy difficulties. It became a burning interest to seek out what was going on in children's out-of-school literacy lives, what might account for early difficulties and, finally, what teachers needed to know to go about changing classroom practices.

Just as I left West Ham to take up a post in Higher Education in 1984, I began reading a new and inspiring American study called *Ways with Words: Language, Life and Work in Communities and Classrooms* by Shirley Brice Heath. In this study, Heath (1983) traces the very different child-rearing practices of two communities living side-by-side in the Appalachians. Through her finely detailed comparison of the linguistic and cultural practices of each community and those expected and practiced in the children's school, Heath goes on to explain to teachers why certain children might be experiencing difficulties and what they need to know in order to devise programmes to foster success. The study resonated with the experiences of many teachers in Britain, including myself. Yet it was clear that the Appalachian Mountains were far from home. It was all too easy to sympathise with the families, to criticise their teachers for their lack of understanding. To do the same in one's own classroom was, however, somewhat different.

Rooted in the local history outlined above and the special way in which I and my family were situated in it, I became passionate about the literacy and learning practices taking place in the lives of children in London's East End and have since completed a number of studies revealing the skills and knowledge of East London families (1994-6, 1999-2000 and 2003-4). Although I couldn't speak Sylheti/Bengali (the first language of many of the participants in my studies), I found myself in collusion with the children and their families against teachers and schools, because we shared, in the widest sense, a common history of prejudice and discrimination. And, as the sub-title to this book suggests, our interpretation of educational ethnography is rooted in the art of collusion.

Such is my answer to the Why? of conducting an ethnographic study. Chapters 2, 3 and 4 will reveal a similar passion by Jean, Chris and Aura as they explain reasons for their choice of study. For the acknowledgement of the self in the study is, we believe, our unique contribution to educational ethnography. It is a contribution which we invite others to make using our experiences outlined in this book as a handbook or guide.

Going about it: what is ethnography in education?

The second part of this chapter moves to the What? of ethnography. It discusses what we believe to be the rules in conducting an ethnography in education and explains why rules might sometimes need to be broken in order to present a case. It begins to answer the question: What should we expect when reading an ethnography? What are the rules as well as constraints of ethnography and what did this mean for us as authors of this book? How did we overcome these constraints? Finally, the chapter explains why we wrote this book and suggests ways in which it may be read.

What should we expect when reading an educational ethnography? Broadly, an ethnography aims to investigate:

- What is occurring
- How it is occurring
- How the participants perceive events
- What is required to participate as a member of that group (school, class, reading group etc.)
- What social and academic learning takes place.

Therefore, an ethnography describes:

- The context or environment
- The group membership (participant or non-participant)
- The specific social interactions
- The product of those interactions – the learning.

That is, an ethnography defines the group, what it means to be a member of the group and what happens through participation in that particular group. Importantly – and difficult for those conducting classroom ethnographies who have been teachers – ethnographers *describe* rather than *judge* what is occurring. They consider recurring patterns of behaviour and infer *the rules for membership* in interactions. Consequently, an ethnographic thesis often comprises the following:

PART ONE

1. A personal, often autobiographical, introduction leading to a definition of the problem or big question to be investigated

2. A pilot study illustrating further the nature of the problem or big question and the subsidiary questions arising.

PART TWO

3. Reference to previous studies and how they have tackled this question, showing that there is clearly a gap in the literature providing a satisfactory answer to your question (this will be yours to fill). This is often (but not always) two chapters of the work.

PART THREE

4. A clear explanation of the methodology and design of the study using various methods of investigation to triangulate your data (participant observation, interviews, case-studies, life-histories etc.)

5. A search for *recurring patterns and events* from the data in order to formulate hypotheses or develop case models grounded in data. This will be repeated with other members or another site to provide trustworthy evidence

6. A refinement of models and hypotheses and how these develop and extend existing theories (referring back to those reviewed previously). Use of your findings to refer to and make suggestions for future educational policy

7. A short conclusion or epilogue summarising the importance of the findings and pointing to future research still needed in the field.

The thesis often comprises two chapters of data analysis (see 5 above), followed by a chapter highlighting key aspects of the evidence for theory building as well as implications for policy.

Ethnography in education: rules, constraints and overcoming constraints

Ethnography is sometimes wrongly understood as being synonymous with qualitative research. This is not the case. Below are what we believe to be some brief but basic rules about ethnography, followed by ways through and around the constraints it may impose.

Rule One: Ethnography is a methodology not a method

A crucial and basic rule is that ethnography is a research *approach*, a *methodology* and *not* simply a method. As such, an ethnography in education may use a whole variety of *different methods*, for example:

- participant observation
- life-histories
- interviews
- case-studies
- surveys and other statistical methods.

Doing an ethnography does *not* mean that quantitative methods such as surveys or statistics cannot be used if they serve to answer the big question of the study.

Rule Two: Ethnography starts with a question not a hypothesis

Ethnographic research always has a big (general) question as the starting-point for investigation. It *does not* start with a hypothesis. The generally accepted procedure is as follows:

- The initial question is followed by substantial field-work in a naturalistic setting; initial field-work is guided by assumptions and hunches

- During field-work, multiple questions and hypotheses are developed arising from the data collected until patterns are discerned to provide an analytic framework; constant feedback from data informs analysis

■ There is a narrowing down of hypotheses to form an argument which is substantiated further through a triangulation of methods

■ On writing up, the aim is to produce 'trustworthy' evidence (Mishler, 1990) through a full and explicit description of the social world in which events take place whilst realising that the reader and researcher share a joint responsibility in interpreting events.

Rule Three: Ethnographers make emic rather than etic observations

Ethnographers make emic observations – those that attempt to adopt the framework and perspective of the participants studied – rather than etic observations – those brought by the researcher's own culture – (Schieffelin and Cochran-Smith, 1984). This is generally made possible by the recognition that the researcher must be *part of the world studied*; that the researcher both changes the situation and is changed by it. Ethnography has been referred to as 'thick description' (Geertz, 1973:9) which is 'our own constructions of other peoples' constructions of what they and their compatriots are up to...'. This recognition thus neatly avoids the dilemma faced by other qualitative work of the observer's paradox, the concern that natural data can never be gathered by the researcher because their very presence causes participants to act unnaturally. Because ethnographers aim to present a 'cultural grammar' (Heath, 1983) of a group, they must make explicit rules that are already implicitly known to the group. Ethnographers must, therefore, remain a stranger within the group as well as being part of it.

It takes little imagination to begin to note some of the contradictions inherent in ethnography for educational research. One problem is that schools themselves are not naturalistic settings and that this will need to be acknowledged in research taking place in classrooms. A second difficulty is that ethnography aims to provide a 'cultural grammar' or description of *a group* not *individuals* within the groups. As in the work of Phillips (1972), Au (1980), Heath (1983) and Michaels (1986) this might well lead to a focus on school failure for certain ethnic or social groups. What about the individual who stands out as different? The child from a disadvantaged group who succeeds against all the odds? This is surely of key interest to most teachers, who want to feel that what they do in classrooms can make a difference. Yet ethnography tends to lead to the view of knowledge as preconstituted through social or cultural background rather than dynamically recreated between individuals.

It was precisely this 'situated' (Cook-Gumperz, 1977) or 'negotiated' (Heap, 1985) knowledge that we wanted to reveal. So how did we go about this without breaking all the rules I've outlined above?

Our own solution was to realise that ethnography as a *single* methodology was simply not sufficient to provide a full and trustworthy answer to our big question. It is fair to say that ethnography provided the wider picture within which our work is situated; an ethnographic lens is needed through which data should be viewed. But each of us needed to search for a second methodology or approach to explain what was happening in the data. And for each the search was a struggle, since it meant stepping outside some of the commonly accepted rules. Gradually, we came to realise that, paradoxically, ethnography itself can be seen to be about rule breaking, since it needs to account for ways in which groups deal with constantly changing cultural practices, practices which we, ourselves, to a greater or lesser extent, may share.

Eventually, and after lengthy and repeated study of the data in the light of the big question posed, we each chose a second methodology in addition to ethnography. This is sometimes referred to as 'multilayering' or a 'multilevel approach' to our analysis. A focus on individual and moment-by-moment teacher/child interaction led me to phenomenology and the use of conversation analysis as an additional methodology (Gregory, 1993). Jean's constant awareness of the social and political backgrounds within which her participants operated led her to choose critical discourse analysis as a second approach (see Chapter Seven); Chris's fascination with the very different yet constant speech patterns of his participants led naturally to the addition of narrative analysis to his work (see Chapter Eight); Aura's concern with the empathy shown between teacher and child encouraged her to search out and find collusion as a research approach (see Chapter Nine). Crucially, these approaches, or methodologies, were sought out in response to the data and the questions posed; data and questions that were left un-answered if the rules of ethnography were to be fully obeyed.

Why this book? Honest experiences with ethnography

General books on research methodology of necessity omit the role of *the self* in the work. Methods of data collection and analysis, rules and procedures, though often clearly and interestingly represented, appear in a void without the context that makes them meaningful. Even if real examples illustrating different methods are used, they come from a number of different authors and, as research students, we consequently lacked empathy for their work.

As writers, we struggled with our own studies and did not see that struggle reflected in general methodology books which portrayed the task as unconvincingly simple. We wanted to read the work of others who had also struggled to find their way through what seemed, at the beginning, to be a chaotic assemblage of observa-tions, interviews, readings and beliefs. We wanted to share in that struggle and to see ways in which it could be resolved. Ultimately, we needed to collude in the secrets of authors who did not just tell us how to conduct a study but shared with us the ups and downs, the blockages and breakthroughs and the messiness of the whole endeavour.

This was our reason for a collaborative writing of the book which, we feel, illustrates the art of collusion on a number of levels: col-lusion with the participants in our studies, with other students en-gaged in a similar task, with our supervisors listening to and advis-ing on the work, with you as readers and, importantly, with each other as co-authors of this book. Ultimately, our collusion is against those promoting simplistic answers to collecting, analysing or interpreting data involving real people. We hope our accounts are honest in revealing our complex journeys through a mass of detail to the final version of the work.

Our aim to evoke empathy as well as provide rigour in our presenta-tion has led us to provide a dual way for the reader in approaching the work. Vertically (chapter by chapter) it takes the reader step by step through the stages of the thesis – or indeed any ethnographic study. Horizontally (author by author) readers can follow the work of each author from conception to completion. With this aim in mind, the style of each author is different, and we make no apology for this. Our ultimate aim and our collaborative contribution to ethnography is to fully legitimise putting the self into the work; to show how personal commitment is not just 'latched on' to the methodology but is wound through it at every step. We hope that this book will enable its readers and future researchers to join us in presenting commitment as a crucial part of ethnographic research.

The following chart shows the organisation of the book – read horizontally (chapters across the rows) to trace the individual projects, or vertically (down the columns) to understand each stage of developing a PhD thesis and writing an educational ethnography:

	Part 1 – beginnnings	Part 2 – pilot study	Part 3 – methodology	Part 4 – conclusions
Jean	Chapter 1	Chapter 4	Chapter 7	Chapter 10
Chris	Chapter 2	Chapter 5	Chapter 8	Chapter 11
Aura	Chapter 3	Chapter 6	Chapter 9	Chapter 12

Notes

1 Interestingly, by 1901 the borough of West Ham (Plaistow, Canning Town and Silvertown) had a population of 267,358, fourteen times greater than its population in 1851. East Ham, which had been a large village of 4,334 in 1871 grew to 96,000: Inwood, S. (1998) *A History of London*, London: Macmillan: 465

2 Joining the armed forces in order not to be a drain on their families. Families were expected to support members not at work (see *City Literacies: Learning to read across generations and cultures*, (Gregory, E. and Williams, A. 2000: London: Routledge, Ch. 3 for personal memories of this)

3 Iser, W. (1974) *The Implied Reader* (Baltimore and London: The John Hopkins University Press) refers to the *implied* reader as one who, although drawn into the action, shades in the outlines suggested by given situations so that these take on a reality of their own. As the reader's imagination animates these outlines, they will, in turn affect the written part of the text

Part one
Beginnings
the story behind the big question

Introduction:
Deep in the soul

Eve Gregory

> We come to every situation with stories; patterns and sequences
> that are built into us. Our learning happens within the experience
> of what important others did. (Bateson, 1979:13)

The situation of writing an ethnographic study is no different
from any other. We come to it with stories, stories that are
grounded in both our own experience and that of important
others in our lives. As such, beginning the actual writing is easy.
Only the story behind the writing might take a while to find. The
first piece of writing I ask of beginner ethnographers (and it should
be done quickly) is to write a short autobiographical piece about the
story behind the study. What is your big question or problem you
want to investigate? Why is it important to you? Why does the story
have to be told? Why should it be *you* who tells it? To embark upon
such a long journey, especially if you are in full-time employment,
necessitates having a passionate interest in the issues studied.
Indeed, the study may remain the one constant, amidst births,
deaths, divorce, job or house change etc. So it often becomes a
comfort, a source of stability in life.

The autobiographical piece often reveals what Margaret Meek
refers to as the 'paradigmatic moment', a magic moment highlighting the essence of the study to come. For Jean, this was the child
from Bangladesh in a British class, hitherto silent and seemingly
unable to write, who suddenly produced pages of writing in his

3

mother tongue. For Chris, it came through Aliki, his Greek participant's one-woman play about a love affair in Cyprus. Aura took
her inspiration from her daughter and other young children's ways
into new languages through stories and literature.

The three chapters in Part One reveal a passion for social justice,
inclusion and exclusion shared by all three authors, a passion that
pervades the book. Yet the roots of this passion and the way in
which they grew were very different in each case. Jean tells how her
fourteen years in West Africa contributed to her sense of difference
upon returning to Britain; a difference that opened her eyes to the
ways in which bilingual children's skills were ignored in the British
school context. Chris describes how 'the seeds of what we are thinking, right now, at this moment, were planted long ago' and tells how
his Irish and Merseyside background, where the men of his family
laboured in the shipyards and docks, sat uneasily with his own experiences of snobbery and exclusivity at grammar school. Aura's
struggle for justice is more explicit. She begins thus: 'Since I was
very young, indeed almost all my life, I have been actively involved
in the peace and social justice movements in Israel...' and continues
by relating her quest to show how bilingualism might promote early
intercultural understanding, possibly against all the odds. All, then,
start their work with a similar ideology but separate into different
directions according to their personal histories and interests.

It is not just personal histories that steer the authors' work however.
The first steps described in Part One also reveal very different per-
sonalities reflected in the practical organisation and management
of the work. All, of course, kept the essential diaries for day-to-day
comments and field-notes from the study. Only Chris, however, the
artist and divergent thinker, gives these particular mention when he
talks of buying beautiful sketch-books and artists' pens and loving
the feel of both in his hands. Jean, the calm, organised perfectionist
shows her meticulous nature and attention to detail as she describes methodically using card indexes for references. Aura, the
poet, came to Britain heavily laden with examples of her children's
work. Instinctively, she understood both children and their teachers
as she interpreted their drawings, writing and spoken text. The
authors show that there is no *right* way of organising data but whatever the approach, authenticity and credibility are key.

Finally, in Chapter One, Jean quotes Woods (1996) who says that one often does research to discover more about oneself. I believe, principally, that one does research in order to learn more about *others*, but in so doing *also* learns more about oneself. The chapters in Part One introduce us to the characters in the studies and to the authors, all of whom accompany us throughout the book.

1

The self in the research: personal and professional starting points

Jean Conteh

The impossibility of objectivity

On a chilly spring day in 1988, I walked out of Bradford Interchange station on my way to a job interview. It was my first visit to the city and first impressions were not encouraging: solid, grey Victorian architecture; bleak, hilly streets; dark skies. I still felt homesick for the tropical sunshine and bright colours of West Africa which I had left not long before, after living there for fourteen years. At the entrance to the station, there were two or three Asian traders, wrapped in warm jackets against the cold. They had collapsible wooden stalls crammed with toys, plastic shoes, hair slides and other colourful bits and pieces. They reminded me of the Fulla traders in Sierra Leone who set up their stalls on every street corner, ready to sell a single cigarette or ten sugar cubes wrapped in a twist of paper at any time of the day or night. The sight of the Bradford traders made me feel a little more cheerful. One of them, perhaps noticing my face relaxing as I walked past, smiled broadly at me. Optimism restored, I went on my way.

Peshkin (1988) writes about the pointlessness of striving for objectivity in educational research. Describing subjectivity as 'a garment that cannot be removed', he suggests that it, like 'other usually unexamined maxims of research', often lies 'inert, unexamined when it counts' in the research process and so its influences are unrecognised and uncontrolled. One of the first ethnography books I read, *Ways with Words* (Heath, 1983) held me enthralled with the way the writer wove her stories of the communities she researched around her 'selves' as researcher, teacher, parent, woman. The first time I read it, I was not consciously thinking of doing ethnographic research. When I did reach that point, I went back to it to try to learn a few things about being a researcher. Subsequently, I was fascinated to read Heath's own critique of her work (Heath, 1993), written in response to an article which proposes different ways of reading *Ways with Words* (deCastell and Walker, 1991). In her 1993 article, Heath describes how she came to regret not including more of her own background in her book in order to 'demystify the work and help future ethnographers' and to draw out

> ... the theoretical links that bring together the anthropologist's 'experiential, embodied knowledge' and the continuing resonances with the printed text as it is read and reread. (page 264)

I completed writing my PhD thesis almost four years ago and, as part of my job now, I supervise PhD students. This has led me to see, again, the vital importance of maintaining the cycles of doing, talking, reading and writing that keep research dynamic and shape its outcomes in the most rigorous and meaningful ways.

But to return to the story – I got the job and went to live in Bradford. After years of living and working as a teacher and teacher-trainer away from England, I was constantly reminded of my own difference. The day after we moved into our new house on the outskirts of the city, our neighbour, a friendly elderly lady who had lived in the street for thirty years, popped in to say hello. She asked where we had come from. I felt hesitant to say 'Sierra Leone', as I thought it might sound odd to her, so I said that we had come from Newcastle, which is where we had been living for the past couple of months. 'Oh,' said Mrs. P., surprised, 'that's a long way'.

Daily life at that time was a series of small revelations. In even apparently trivial ways, I was very conscious of the gaps in my knowledge of the minutiae of the English culture of the mid-1980s; I remember, for example, having to ask someone what a filofax was. In professional contexts, I was acutely aware of the ways in which I seemed to perceive things differently from the other teachers I came into contact with. I felt something of an outsider and went through a period of feeling really quite alienated and de-skilled, something I have since found is not uncommon in people moving between very different working contexts within a profession. With the advantages of hindsight, I can see that such feelings fed my motivation for undertaking ethnographic research in the contexts in which I was working.

At the same time as recognising and working with subjectivities in the way that Peshkin describes, the ethnographer has to work to maintain, rather than eliminate, the insider/outsider duality. Mehan (1981) speaks elegantly of the 'stances' which ethnographers must take, contrasting 'anthropological' ethnographers working in exotic settings in distant lands with those working in more 'local' settings:

> The ethnographer working in a foreign land is attempting to make the strange familiar, while the ethnographer in local scenes must reverse the process and make the familiar strange in order to understand it. (page 47)

Ely *et al* (1997:32) also discuss the notion of stance in qualitative research, describing the 'complex network of belief systems and positions embedding, superimposing and undergirding any research project'. They point out that the aim is not to eradicate any biases which such positions may lead to, but to reveal them and to acknowledge their effects in the research. So it is important to understand yourself. Reading the introduction to Woods' (1996) eloquent book about the 'art' of teaching gave me the confidence to see how autobiographical exploration and writing is not self-indulgent, but an excellent way to begin to understand the problem and define the important research questions which will help to illuminate it.

Learning from the children: difference or deficit?

The job was as a Section 11-funded language support teacher. The school was one of the original Board Schools built with solid optimism in Bradford at the end of the 19th century. It was a huge, barracks-like building on a steep hill. For the first few weeks I worked there, it seemed as if a cutting wind blew incessantly across the sloping concrete playground, stirring up not autumn leaves but litter and gritty dust. The vast majority of the children were of Pakistani Muslim heritage and had Mirpuri Punjabi as their first language.

When I got to know them, I enjoyed their company and found them alert and lively. They reminded me in many ways of children in Sierra Leone. They were very aware of the world around them and full of interesting and – at times – startlingly perceptive opinions. They told me all kinds of fascinating things about Pakistan (about which I knew very little) and their extended family networks, which ranged from West Yorkshire and various other parts of Britain to Canada, east Africa and the north of Pakistan. They showed a sophisticated awareness of language and cultural diversity. Several children spotted immediately that my accent was different from most other teachers in the school. Why, they asked, did I say 'book' in the way I did, and they imitated my north eastern diphthong. I told them that this was because I came from outside Yorkshire. They spotted that my pronunciation of the word was the same as another staff member's, who also came from Newcastle.

But in their classrooms, things were different. Once inside, some of the children seemed hardly able to talk at all and did not seem to make any academic progress between Year 5 and Year 8. The teachers in the school were genuinely concerned about their pupils and their problems, but nothing seemed to help. A great deal of time and effort was spent in trying to compensate for what were perceived as the children's deficits, cognitive, social and cultural. As the National Curriculum was introduced, the problems seemed to grow worse. We struggled to plan activities about the Victorians or the Vikings, or whatever subject was prescribed for the particular point we had reached in the children's progress through the cumbersome files of the curriculum's first incarnation. We tried to come to terms with the welter of paperwork that seemed to be called for. Despite our efforts, self-fulfilling prophecies seemed inevitably to be realised and the culture of low expectations in the school was reinforced.

In Peshkin's terms (1988), the 'Justice-Seeking I' of my subjectivity was aroused; I felt distress and anger at the disparaging of the community with which I had begun to identify. But unlike Peshkin, I was not researching the community – at this time, I was not aware of how this could be done and probably could not have done it anyway, as I felt too close to it and too personally implicated. Instead, what I did was to 'strike back' (Geertz, 1973) through writing. I wrote a short article about some of my perceptions of the bilingual children and what I perceived to be their hidden potential and sent it off to the only journal I knew which might be interested. I still have the warm and encouraging letter which I received back from the editor, almost by return of post. Not only did she publish the article (Conteh, 1990), but she also told me how important she thought it was. Her positive response was a key factor for me in moving towards carrying out my research, though it was still to be several years before it began.

A paradigmatic moment

In the school, it was not all doom and gloom. Some children did succeed, and did so magnificently. One such was a boy who arrived from Bangladesh a few months after I began working at the school. Mashuq was nine years old and, on the death of his father in Bangladesh, had come with his mother to live with an uncle's family in Bradford. He was tall for his age, smart and confident-looking. He could speak almost no English, and he tagged onto my group of children, those who were deemed by their class teachers to be in need of language support. I really did not know how to teach him. He sat mutely in the circle of nine or ten children round our large table, attentive but apparently uncomprehending. I had begun doing some work on stories with the group. I told them traditional stories from Sierra Leone, then the children drew pictures of their favourite parts of the story and I scribed their sentences describing the pictures. The home-school liaison officer got interested and joined in, so I asked her if she could do some Urdu translations for us. She began chatting with the children in Punjabi and answering their questions while she did so. Through all this, Mashuq sat calmly, occasionally talking in Bangla to the only other Bangladeshi-heritage child in the group, a thin, quiet little boy called Tanveer who never seemed to show much interest in the things we did.

A few days later, one of those rare but unforgettable magic moments in teaching occurred. Mashuq walked into my room and handed me several sheets of paper covered in neat, closely written script. I did not recognise the script, but it happened that there was a teacher from the Inter-Faith Centre in school that day, taking a special assembly for the handful of Hindu children, of whom Mashuq was one. I showed the teacher the papers and he told me that the script was Bangla. The teacher got interested and talked with Mashuq for quite a while in Bangla. It turned out that the sheets contained a story from Bangladesh that Mashuq had written out the night before, inspired by my Sierra Leonean stories, which Tanveer had retold to him in Bangla. The Hindu teacher told me that Mashuq's written Bangla was very good and that he had clearly reached a high level in school before leaving Bangladesh. This information had never been revealed to anyone in his new, English school. After that, via Tanveer, I asked Mashuq to write stories in Bangla as well as to give us translations of the African stories when he could. We made trilingual books, in English, Urdu and Bangla; I still have some of them. Mashuq recorded some Bangla stories onto audiotape which Tanveer and the other Bangla-speaking children in the school loved to listen to. Within six months, Mashuq was a confident reader and writer of English. Tanveer wasn't doing too badly, either.

At the time, I knew very little about bilingualism and biliteracy, and did not understand how it was that Mashuq was able to learn to read English so quickly. His success made me interested in finding out more, and I began to read about the issues. I discovered Cummins' 'interdependence' hypothesis (Cummins, 1984) and all the debates about bilingualism and special education, as well about the role of story in children's learning (e.g. Wells, 1986). But my main sense of what was so important for Mashuq was what I would now call his identity. He himself had taken control of his own learning.

His calmness and self-confidence, and his apparent ability to mediate the vastly different worlds of home and school which he inhabited, were the attributes which seemed to me to be the most powerful factors for his success. When I began working as a teacher-trainer and talking to groups of students about learning to read, I found myself telling and re-telling Mashuq's story. It contained for me all the elements that illustrated what it entailed to be a successful learner of English as an additional language – or any kind of learner for that matter. What I had done with the stories had possibly helped, but the most important factor was Mashuq himself. When I began to synthesise the theoretical framework about language and learning which was to underpin my research, I realised that Mashuq had taught me a lot about what needed to be included in theorising and researching models of learning.

Language, power and making connections

Around this time, as happens so often, events outside the classroom began to have an unsettling effect on life in school. In January 1989, the 'Rushdie affair' erupted. A copy of *The Satanic Verses* was burnt – in front of the TV cameras – in the centre of the city, Salman Rushdie was denounced by the Imams in the local mosques and for a while the name of Bradford hit international headlines. These events had a disturbing effect locally. Racist graffiti appeared on several buildings on the route I took to school and elsewhere in the local area, there were a few scuffles on the streets in the neighbourhood and there seemed to be more aggression than usual in the playground. One day in the classroom, I asked a child to spread out newspapers on the tables so that we could get the paints out. She opened out the paper and, noticing a photo of Rushdie on one of the pages, dropped it onto the floor in horror. Any religious issues underpinning the events had soon been swallowed up in the political games which the various local players indulged to the detriment of community harmony.

Like many people, I was very troubled by all of this. To refer to Peshkin again, it was evidence, perhaps, of some aspect of my 'Ethnic Maintenance I' being challenged. Though not a Muslim, I found it disturbing and dangerous that Islam seemed to have become a source of political point scoring. Before I went to live in

Bradford, my experience of Islam had been as an interesting part of the colourful backdrop to everyday life in Sierra Leone, through hearing the call to prayer blare out on crackly cassette tapes from minarets early in the morning, through being invited to Eid cele- brations and watching large crowds of people in elegant robes gathering for prayers in the town where I lived. About 50 per cent of the population of Sierra Leone are identified as Muslim but – at the time I lived there – they were in many ways indistinguishable from those who practised other religions. Indeed, Islam seemed to be just another part of the dynamic mix of cultural, social and religious practices that made up daily life for Sierra Leoneans. It was not the stern, forbidding code of behaviour that many people seemed to construct it as – on both sides of the debate – in Bradford. I was disturbed by the negativity such viewpoints seemed to generate.

One day in school, I was sitting musing over such issues while I supervised a group of children carrying out a task. As I half-listened to their quiet chatter, I thought I heard a word that I recognised. The children were talking to each other in Punjabi, and I asked them what they had said. At first, they were puzzled and a little suspicious about why I wanted to know, but they soon overcame their hesita- tions and identified the word for me:

> It's 'duniya', Miss. It means 'the world'.

I could hardly believe my ears. I knew the word *duniya* in two other languages, Sierra Leone Krio (Fyle and Jones, 1980), and Mende (Innes, 1969) an indigenous language of Sierra Leone, part of the Persian-related Mande group which spread into West Africa from the Islamic north. There were numerous expressions in Sierra Leone which people used to declare their patient, but ironic, accep- tance of things they could not control, and *eh, duniya!* was one of them. From what the children told me, it could be used in similar metaphorical ways in Punjabi. I had made a connection. I began to understand that, for the children I was teaching, Islam wasn't a cold and forbidding religion, or the object of a political game. Just as for Muslim children in Sierra Leone, it was part of their everyday lives and ways of doing things, a set of cultural and social practices that shaped their experiences. Language itself is a cultural practice, and reflects most of the things we do in our everyday lives. There are many words like *duniya*, which have travelled throughout the Islamic world, and been appropriated at various times in history by people whose external circumstances may be very different, but whose lives are moulded by essentially the same needs, beliefs, desires and emotions.

For all children, moving from the cultural and social worlds of home into those of school entails learning a new language, the one which mediates their transition from 'children into pupils' (Willes, 1983). The processes involved have been described by many writers. Setbacks can occur in the co-construction of meanings, even in the most propitious of circumstances. I remember my daughter's first primary teacher in England telling me about a small incident that had puzzled her. She had asked my daughter, who was then aged seven and had only spent a few weeks in this particular classroom, to balance a set of scales. The teacher did not understand why all she got in return was a confused look. When she described to me later what had happened, I realised what the problem had been. In Sierra Leone, to balance something means to carry it on your head. It is not surprising then that, in this small classroom incident, the negotiation of meaning between teacher and pupil had not been successful.

Similar mis-communications occurred frequently between the Pakistani-heritage children in school and their teachers. Struggling to express themselves or to understand teacher talk in English, they often became incoherent, leaving teachers confused about what they were trying to say. I remember Tahmina, an unhappy little girl who had not been in England very long and seemed to be finding it hard to adapt. One day, I was trying to talk to her, and, showing her a black-and-white drawing of a goat, I asked her what it was. 'Is it a boy a girl?' she asked, a perfectly reasonable question in terms of Punjabi, a language in which speakers need to know the sex of the animal in order to name it correctly – and, most likely, understandable too in terms of Tahmina's lived experience in Pakistan. At the same time, the children's positive and active engagement with different culturally based ways of describing the world was very apparent. They sometimes invented words and expressions in English which reflected their attempts to describe things which were important to them; one such example was the way they talked about 'sister-cousins' and 'brother-cousins' to describe their relatives who would be described by most native speakers of English simply as 'cousins'. It was important to them to find a way to make English as descriptive of families and family relationships as Punjabi is, with its wide range of words for family members of many possible permutations.

Such examples, besides showing some of the ways in which negotiation of meanings can go awry in classrooms, also show how language development and learning must be seen as cultural as well as cognitive. I have written about these issues elsewhere (Conteh, 2003). As long ago as 1973, Halliday suggested that, for many children, their problems with language arise because they are required to accept 'a stereotype of language that is contrary to the insights he (*sic*) has gained from his own experience' (page 11). I argued in my PhD thesis that children's failure in school was often not as a result of any deficit embodied within themselves, rather the causes were systemic, representing, in Trueba's (1989:19) terms:

> ... not an individual failure, but a failure of the social system to provide the child with the opportunity for social intercourse ...

Delpit (1995:45) similarly talks about learners who are not 'allowed to be themselves in a system designed for others' in classrooms where their home and community knowledge is not recognised and valued.

The big problem

But I did not know any of this until much later. When I left the school after three years to work in primary teacher training, I took with me a problem, a big question I wanted to answer. I could not understand why the children whom I found so interesting to talk to outside their classrooms were failing in such a serious way inside them. It was by no means a new problem, or one confined to the school I had been working in. As I began to visit different classrooms – in other countries as well as nearer to home – in my role as teacher-trainer, I realised the complexity of the issues. I saw that, to research my problem, I would need to find ways to encapsulate these complexities. I was tired of hearing about the failures and underachievements of ethnic minority children, and decided that I wanted somehow to focus on success. The word 'culture' kept floating up from the pages I was reading. It seemed significant, but I did not know how. This was an early attempt to formulate some questions about my problem:

1. *What factors contribute to a positive learning culture?*

2. *How do teachers establish this positive learning culture in their classrooms?*

3. *What roles do children play in co-constructing this learning culture?*

4. *What is the importance of language in all this?*

My personal and professional selves were about to take on new subjectivities as researcher and ethnographer, and the catalyst for this was my first meeting with Eve Gregory. Again, it was the personal reassurance of the importance of the work that counted. In a letter she sent me in September 1995, Eve wrote:

> ... you must not give up ... your work is very important. We have so little research available in this whole area and you have already made excellent beginnings.

After such affirmation, I took what was possibly the most decisive step yet towards signing up to do a part-time PhD – I went out and bought a big red notebook in which to write my field notes and the largest card index file I could find to start filing my bibliography.

2

Instinctive continuity:
autobiography, ethnography
and personal commitment
from the beginning

Chris Kearney

The past is not dead. It is not even past. William Faulkner

...as we know, all theory has its roots, in one way or another in autobiography. David Morley

Embryonic journey: how I got started on the PhD

Let's begin at the end. Somebody said that a piece of writing is never finished – it is just abandoned. It's also not clear where it starts. Tracing the beginning of a piece of writing, and especially a major piece like a doctoral thesis, is difficult. I can't remember clearly when I made the decision to start or why. In some ways it is the culmination of a lifetime's interest and study. A student asked Jean how long she took to write hers and she replied, 'Forty-nine years.' I was even older when I completed mine and I think that I needed that amount of experience. I'm sure this isn't true for everyone but, for me, it came at the right time.

A series of seemingly disconnected events led me to take the first formal steps towards enrolling and I was fortunate in having several people who were able to guide me. In 1994 I was running a Licensed Teacher Programme at Middlesex University on a series of one-year contracts and I had the vague suspicion that a PhD would help me towards a more secure employment. Coincidentally, a recently appointed research professor took a genuine interest in my writing and encouraged me further in this direction. So I approached Tony Burgess who had supervised my MA dissertation at the Institute five years before. At that stage I wanted to investigate the notion of reflective practice through a study of the life histories of mentor teachers we were working with on the Licensed Teacher Programme. This was a long way from ethnography.

My direction changed when I was appointed to lead the Primary PGCE Programme at Goldsmiths College in early 1995. I discovered that funding was not available for me to study at the Institute, but that there were people who could supervise me at Goldsmiths. Tony recommended Eve Gregory and I met her shortly afterwards. She was interested in supervising me but did not know very much about mentoring. Her area of expertise is ethnography in education. I talked to her about my MA and my interest in ideas of culture and identity and the link between identity and motivation to succeed in school. It was here that we found common ground.

Before leaving Middlesex, Richard Andrews, the research professor, invited me to take part in a conference he was organising on the post-Dearing Review of the National Curriculum. I agreed to submit a paper on the effect of the changes on the education of bilingual pupils. Eve read drafts of the paper and provided encouraging feedback. At the end of my conference presentation, an ex-student came up to express her interest in my talk and told me how it resonated with her own experience as a Greek Cypriot child growing up in East London. She also gave me her phone number and asked me to get in touch if I wanted to do any further research in the area.

This changed the direction completely. However, I didn't abandon my original idea altogether. I realised that it may be a good idea to collect life stories of academically successful bilinguals, especially since much of the research and official documents concentrated on underachievement. It was closely linked to my MA dissertation, part of which had been a case study of a successful bilingual child.

I also realised that life histories were not very far from ethnography, which was Eve's area of study. After all doesn't ethnography always draw on the life experiences of their informants?

Why autobiography?
Before I went any further with this, Eve asked me to write an auto-biographical account of how I became interested in this area. This kind of personal involvement in your own research is anathema to those academics who see it as self-indulgent and unscientific. However, since Polyani published *Personal Knowledge* in 1958 the emphasis in academic research has been shifting steadily.

In *Works and Lives: The Anthropologist as Author*, Geertz (1988) debunks the myth that ethnography is a precise and objective science. Through textual analysis he reveals the personal commitments, obsessions and idiosyncratic modes of expression in the works of Levi-Strauss, Ruth Benedict, Evans-Pritchard and Malinowski. In Malinowski's case a major scandal erupted when his diaries revealed a less than scrupulous approach to his source materials. In the age which celebrated objectivity, personal commitment led to less than honest work. More obviously and more recently Shirley Brice Heath (1983) scarcely bothered to conceal the autobiographical inspiration of *Ways with Words*. It is now widely accepted that autobiographical approaches to ethnography can be useful and indeed healthy.

What is a PhD? What is *my* PhD?
As I see it, the kernel of any research project, such as a PhD, lies in a peculiar amalgam of long-term obsessions and random happenings, which crystallise the central problem in specific and concrete ways. These random events could be, for instance, a chance meeting, a sentence in a book, a devastating news story, a fragment of conversation overheard on a bus or train, a deeply irritating statement by someone on the radio, a problem at work, our reaction to particular government policies or initiatives. The list is almost endless and I guess mine was, at various stages, a combination of most the above. Such moments sometimes force us into action against some perceived injustice or fill us with a desire to puzzle something out. They situate us personally and politically. It's my belief that

doctoral studies should begin when something is deeply lodged in a person's own experience of the world, which puzzles or annoys or intrigues them. But I also believe that those things are already in place. The seeds of what we are thinking, right now, at this moment, were planted long ago. The questions that bother us now are not new. If there was one central idea which influenced me throughout my own research it was the one articulated so well by Antonio Gramsci, which I stumbled across in Edward Said's book *Orientalism*, (1987) whilst I was pursuing my MA course (I've never been able to trace the original):

> The starting point of critical elaboration is the consciousness of what one really is, and is knowing thyself as a product of the historical processes to date which have deposited within you an infinity of traces, without leaving an inventory: therefore it is imperative at the outset to compile such an inventory. (Cited in Said, 1987: 25)

All I'm saying here is that a PhD is such a major piece of writing that it is necessary to make explicit what drew you into the area at the outset. It forms the cornerstone of the thesis. In fact, after completing the formal proposal required by the college, this was the first piece of writing I attempted. Eve insisted upon it.

The uses of autobiography

Writing that autobiographical introduction made the relationship between my life and the work explicit to me. It forced me to reflect deeply and systematically upon my own intellectual development, drawing many disparate strands together. Perhaps, for the first time in my life, I could actually see where my interest in multilingualism and cultural diversity originated. In hindsight it helped shape the work and led me steadily towards the big question. My family had also been immigrants, from Ireland, and as I was growing up I realised that I had peculiar ambivalences about my own heritage. For some time these had been central themes in my own work. For me one of the greatest joys of doing the doctoral thesis was the surprise of such discoveries and their connection to play and creativity.

The second thing it did was to put my reading into perspective. I had already completed a post-graduate diploma course at Middlesex University in 1979 and an MA at the Institute of Education about a decade later. Those courses also drew on my passion for literature and especially poetry, which I had studied for my first degree. They also sowed the seeds of my interest in sociolinguistics, which struck deep chords with my own childhood in a working class neighbourhood on Merseyside in the 1950s. My father, both of my grandfathers and most of my uncles had worked in the shipyards and the docks. These experiences had galvanised my distaste for social injustice and exclusion, which had been refined during my time at a grammar school where I experienced snobbery and exclusivity at first hand.

Keeping track: note taking and the supervisor's role

I can't overemphasise the importance of the supervisor's role in the direction of one's thesis. I was lucky to find a supervisor who was sympathetic to my ideas, my eclectic reading and my quirky way of expressing myself. In other words, she was interested in enabling me to develop my own ideas and my own voice and not forcing her own directions and preoccupations upon me. Having said that, she would advise and guide me and ask me to undertake certain tasks at certain times and get me to meet deadlines, whilst being understanding about the inevitable curves life throws at you from time to time. She knew when to apply pressure and when to lay off. She also made it clear that I should have some systematic way of recording my thoughts and my reading. Her own approach was box-index files with notes on her reading. It was well ordered and systematic. I tried it for about a month and found that it did not suit my own style or approach. I prefer narrative approaches and probably always have. I find it easier also to retrieve information this way. My mnemonic system consists of associating what I am reading with other signposts in my life: events that happened at work or with family and friends; what I have been reading in the widest sense; even particular pieces of music I am listening to. I can then usually find what I need quickly and accurately. This led me back to my use of a journal. As time went on I learned to note more and more precisely the details of particular quotations, including page numbers and the publisher and where published. This saved enormous amounts of time later on.

Using journals

The journey through the PhD is never smooth. We all encounter difficulties and frustrations at every stage. I am really glad that I kept a journal throughout. I can't recommend it strongly enough. I used mine for a multitude of purposes: for venting my frustrations, for keeping a record of my reading, taking notes in networks, workshops and conferences I attended, to jot down thoughts and to draft and rehearse my writing for conference papers and the thesis. They have been an invaluable resource for me and so far I have been lucky enough not to lose any of them.

Whilst doing the MA I had used journals. At that stage they were black Rowney sketchbooks. I liked the size and the feel of them. Using Faber Castell's artists' pens made writing a physical pleasure. Again this will be more important to some people than others. But you need to get your own system and approach. In my journal I would write about the books I was reading at the time, peppered with quotations which moved, intrigued or irritated me. I would also note how I felt the writing was going at particular times and why. I registered my successes and frustrations. I would also carry them around so that if I had an idea or a question I could note that too. Sometimes this would mean extended passages.

Writing is a strange phenomenon. Sometimes I don't know that I think something until it's written down. Sometimes I get so carried away I'm not at all sure that it is me who has written it at all. Those are really great moments. When I look at it again later, sometimes I find it is insightful and usable. At other times it appears trite and worthless. It means, however, that when I am preparing a chapter, I can often write directly from my journal. I realise that not everyone has this approach, but you need to have a supervisor who will allow you to develop the ways you find the most productive and creative.

As I'm writing this I am referring to those parts of the journals which deal with the early stages of my work on the PhD. Reading them again I am reminded that the struggles and frustrations I was experiencing were not only to do with the study itself but existed in other areas of my life too. In some ways concentrating on the study helped me to cope with those external pressures and quite often provided temporary escape and respite from them. The other thing

I notice is how they articulate the interests and problems I am still pursuing. Of course this is with the benefit of hindsight. They didn't appear so clear and straightforward at the time.

Supportive networks and audiences for the work

Writing can also be a frustrating, lonely and isolated business particularly in the final stages and I will talk about this more fully in a later chapter. Yet from the beginning stages our supervisor sought to minimise this for us. As you will notice, we all have overlapping interests and she had set up a network of people who were at various stages of study for the PhD or had recently completed them. It is an intercollegiate network with students and tutors from various colleges of London University; Goldsmiths, University College and King's. Later we were joined by others from the Institute of Education. This meant that we were always sharing ideas. If the autobiographical introduction helped to give us a sense of purpose and direction, then the network gave us a sense of audience.

The way the sessions were structured helped us to clarify and rehearse our arguments. Introducing ourselves, we were encouraged to talk about our jobs and interests. Others in the group would ask clarifying questions and sometimes suggest other angles or alternatives which were always helpful. Without this I think the whole process would have been more difficult. The approach also helped us to link the work we were doing to our private and professional lives.

For each session, one or two of us would prepare a presentation of our work in progress. For some sessions, someone who had just completed their thesis gave us an account of how they got through the experience; the problems and dilemmas they faced, and how they resolved them. It was extremely helpful to realise that they too had times when they were stuck or had false starts or disappeared up cul-de-sacs. Moreover they would share with us books that had been helpful or meaningful to them. There was a great deal of sharing of stimulating ideas and reading in the sessions. I was given many new angles on culture and identity and insights about my own work that would have otherwise eluded me. I always came away with ideas of how I could continue. I learned a great deal about the area of ethnography from my colleagues. On reflection, this saved me a great deal of time in libraries, particularly at the beginning.

A note on reading

Obviously all this existed alongside individual tutorials with our supervisor. The network meetings meant that Eve had a detailed knowledge of our work in progress so that the tutorials were much more concerned with theoretical reading and writing. What was helpful for me was that, very early on, she sketched out what was involved in a PhD and how it differed from an MA. From her own experience she stressed the importance of settling upon a methodological approach. The tutorials allowed me to talk about my own influences, particularly the work of Vygotsky (1978,1986), Bakhtin (1981, 1984, 1986) and Geertz (1973, 1983, 1988, 1995) whose work remains pivotal in my own thinking. On the other hand she recommended several books and articles which were key texts for her. Some of these were also important to me and I'll mention a few. Hazel Francis' (1993) phenomenographic approaches to interviewing provided me with a clear starting point for the interviews I conducted. Gregory Bateson's (1979) view that ethnographic research was a quest for 'the pattern that connects' was an important consideration in my analysis of the interviews. I also admired the way that he could express complex ideas in straightforward ways. Just before I began the interviews the direction of the thesis was strongly influenced by a talk given at one of the network meetings. Susi Long had recently completed her study and shared with us the ideas of Van Maanen (1988). This provided a good starting point for me. It also led me back to the ideas and reading I had come across in my MA dissertation. I was therefore able to consolidate what I had read from cultural studies, particularly the works of Stuart Hall. However, the real catalyst for my own thinking was Ien Ang's paper, *On not Speaking Chinese* (1994) which illustrated, in an autobiographical way, the complexity of the problem of identity which I felt lay at the heart of my own research.

For me, the understanding that came from my doctoral study emerged gradually as a photographic image emerges slowly in the developing tray. I was motivated to find realistic ways in which teachers could link with the cultural and linguistic knowledge that bilingual students brought to the classroom. I knew that it linked in some way with their collective and personal sense of identity. I wanted to find out exactly how this fitted together. But I didn't know how it would finish up. And it didn't really matter at that stage. I was on a journey.

Writing the autobiographical section

So now the groundwork was laid. The autobiographical introduction was designed to lead me to the questions I wanted to explore. From my journals I can see that it did that in concrete and practical ways. I want to explore that connection in the final section of this chapter. But first I will consider the finished product as it appeared in my thesis. What follows is an extract from the autobiographical section in the introductory chapter, which I wrote relatively quickly and which did not change significantly from my first draft. After that I will trace how it led initially to the content and structure of the interviews I conducted and ultimately to my big question.

> My interest in ... questions [of culture, language and identity] can be traced back to my own childhood and adolescence. My own confusions were real despite my growing up through a period of relative affluence and being relatively successful within the state education system.
>
> In terms of my own identity I feel I have inherited sets of paradoxes and ambivalences, which are by no means rare in the modern world. My cultural heritage is predominantly Catholic Irish. From my earliest glimmerings of memory, this was apparent through the litanies of family histories, the stories and the humour. Despite this, we by no means participated in an active Irish culture. Although I was christened a Catholic, my parents scarcely attended mass and I was sent to non-denominational state schools. The only words of Gaelic I know are *Pogue Mahone* and these were taught to me by a roguish uncle, who had very little of the tongue himself. We never attended any social gatherings or belonged to political organisations, yet I knew about the violence of the Orange parades in Liverpool and heard of the heartless exploits of the black and tans and even of Cromwell's crimes at Drogheda, long before I understood their significance.

As I have grown older I have found myself increasingly drawn to Irish music and literature and am proud of that part of my heritage; proud to belong to a culture which since 1169 has been invaded and oppressed, but never truly conquered. It is only relatively recently that I visited Ireland for the first time, since my sister now lives there and my mother lived there for the last years of her life. Yet I still have no desire to be part of it. So many things irritate and depress me about it; parts of which I continue to find in myself, from time to time. An insincere gregariousness and forced hospitality. A maudlin sense of self-pity. Compulsory gaiety and good humour in public places. An oversensitivity at the comments of others. The list is almost endless.

This complexity is compounded by issues of class, which set up similar paradoxical reactions within me. My grandparents were Irish lower middle class. I suppose they would have had much in common with those which Joyce delineates so vitally in *Dubliners.* Quite different from their English counterparts. By the time my parents were growing up during the years following the Great War, they were poor. Ruined by a combination of poor financial judgment, alcohol and unremitting unemployment. Both my parents left school when they were fourteen. I grew up in what would have been described as a working class neighbourhood.

Irvine Terrace in New Ferry was a row of ten three-storey Victorian houses. They had large rooms and had once belonged to middle class people. They crouched on the edge of the Wirral bank of the Mersey, between Bromborough Docks and Cammell Laird shipyards. By the time my parents rented the top two floors of number two, the sea had already begun to reclaim the gardens. As children we played on the broken sea wall. The most derelict part served as everything from a climbing frame to a shop counter. A place for fighting and role play. It was here that I began to learn that class was not so simple and that community can be a misleading term. Some of the most affluent people in that area were fiercely working class and some of the poorest had 'ideas above their station.'

Although they were never parochial in their attitudes, both my parents had great faith in education, to provide a way out of poverty. With their encouragement, both my sister and I were successful. Still I didn't feel totally comfortable at Wirral Grammar School. Most of the children I had played with in primary school went on to the secondary modern school. But gradually I made new friends and like many of my generation found common ground through the music of the sixties and the styles of expression which grew out of it. Reading Salinger was a profoundly liberating experience. It seemed to free me from the constraints of the past. This continued throughout my time at North Western Polytechnic, where the attractions of the counter culture focused our attention on a range of radical possibilities informed by a tradition which went back past the beat poets, to Dickinson, Pound, Yeats, Beaudelaire, Rilke and Blake. It was an era full of contradictions. Radical, egalitarian politics coexisted (often uneasily) with eastern and western mysticism. It is difficult at this point to describe with any conviction the sense of possibility and optimism which characterise that era.

This was the personal baggage I brought to my work as a teacher in Hackney in the early 1970s and later in Tottenham. Here I encountered a range of further complexities and contradictions. Many of the children seemed alienated from the work we were trying to do. At that stage few teachers had much knowledge of the lives of the children in our classrooms. It was through this experience that many teachers began to discover other ways forward. Looking back, many of our approaches were naive and often patronising. But we were learning.

I then linked this autobiographical piece with some of the major theoretical influences upon my thinking, mentioned earlier in this chapter. It is uncanny for me to realise now that most of the central ideas for my finished thesis are contained in embryonic form in this short chapter. It seems to be the DNA print for the rest.

From the autobiography to the interviews

With hindsight I can say that the autobiographical section functioned on several levels. It was a place I could return to when the work threatened to veer off course. Secondly it led me to the areas which interested me. In an entry written shortly after I had completed the chapter, I noted in my journal:

There must be sets of interviews (not single interviews) which deal with distinct phases:

- pre-school experiences
- early schooling to 11
- secondary
- tertiary and beyond

Themes will include family loyalties, fitting in or opting out, educational dilemmas, parents' views on education, narratives of education, pivotal experiences, individual teachers' actions, internal motives and motivations, achievements, effects of achievements, disappointments, betrayals and regrets. Gains. Points of no return. Theories of teaching and learning. Feelings now.

How much is to be prepared in advance? How much spontaneous? What do I need to read?

This will give a flavour of the notebooks. But reading them now I realise how much the autobiographical piece had sharpened my own intuitions. Most of the intentions outlined in these notes were achieved. Obviously there were also some significant changes. The first was that there was only sufficient time for single interviews. The notes were obviously written in preparation for a tutorial with Eve, because they are immediately followed by four names and phone numbers of people she knew who she thought might want to take part. I guess this is another facet about such research. The networks I talked about earlier ensured that there were always people who would know others who could be contacted to participate in the research. As things fell out, only one of the people suggested by Eve took part in the research.

The suggestions for reading she gave at the tutorial are works by Francis (1993), Silverman (1993) and Alasuutari (1995). They all come from the field of ethnographic and cultural studies methodology. I didn't realise this came so early in the project. They were certainly helpful in focusing the approaches I was to take and in devising the kind of open-ended questioning I was to use in the initial interviews.

After compiling a list of possible questions and openings I make several observations on my reading of Hazel Francis (1993) who:

... prompted a few more ideas about the conduct of the research:

- I will be upfront about my own curiosity in this (research) and it will be a series of conversations rather than interviews. No preconceptions. Or patterns to force the thoughts and recollections into.

  - (be) open to pursue avenues set up by them

■ they will have editorial control over the material

■ we will begin with individual interviews and later meet as a group so that I can tease out the patterns, similarities, discontinuities and implications for the future, especially as they are involved in teaching/education from different standpoints

■ experience within the profession

■ status within the profession.

Reflections on the journals

It has been a slightly eerie experience reading the journals at this distance. Those sections were written eight years ago. What surprises me is how little was wasted or rejected in the final thesis. I am also amazed at how many times I revisit the same themes and questions in slightly different ways and how gradually the thesis built as a whole. For me everything was happening at once. I was reading consistently and continually, but I was also asking myself endless questions from different perspectives, both practical and philosophical, and endlessly rehearsing the way I wanted to express myself. The questions I was asking myself then became the questions I was going to ask the participants.

Then I had the dilemma of how I was going to approach 'Aliki', who offered to be interviewed. I wanted to allow her to tell her story in her own way, yet I also wanted to cover certain topics I was interested in. I made the decision to send her a list of the questions, on the understanding that the conversation would be far less structured. As it happened I needn't have agonised so much since the interview went well.

Paradigmatic moments

In her introduction Eve talks about paradigmatic moments: those episodes or chance remarks which emerge and crystallise the problem in a clear way. They are the real turning points. Aliki was a great storyteller and our conversation threw up at least three such paradigmatic moments, which caused me to re-evaluate what I wanted to know.

The first paradigmatic moment came when she told me that no teacher had explicitly built upon her own linguistic and cultural background, yet if they had it would have had a dramatically positive effect upon her sense of self esteem. As I shall explain later, this was a common pattern. Therefore it took away the major objective of my initial plan for the study; the one in which I wanted to discover how teachers built upon their home backgrounds and how this contributed to their academic success.

The second paradigmatic moment was the revelation of profound ambivalences towards several aspects of her heritage culture. Gender issues were most obviously at the base of these discomforts. Again this was common to several of the participants.

The final point was a story she told of writing a one woman play about her culture in her final year as a student on a performing arts degree course. It revealed how complex and contradictory the strands of her identity were. This led me to wonder how people in her position construct such identities. Her story became a central example in papers I presented at conferences. Once again, I had to follow a quite different path. Things were getting nice and complicated.

3

The text and the context
– some introductions

Aura Mor-Sommerfeld

Ginge da ein Wind
Könnte ich ein Segel stellen
Wäre da kein Segel
Machte ich eines aus Stecken und Plane.
Bertold Brecht, *Die Auswanderung der Dichter.*

If there were a wind,
I could hoist a sail.
If there were no sail,
I could use a stick and a rag.
Bertolt Brecht, *Exile of the Poets.*

What was there, what is there, in Bertolt Brecht's lines, that made me adopt them as *my motto*? Is it really so simple – just the wind, and/or a stick, and a rag? I thought then, and I still think that these lines tell a pure story. I think that, in the simplest way, these lines reveal and state a problem but they also suggest a solution. And they do so as many stories do. They don't just tell a story – *they are* the story.

* * *

My work deals with language, literacy and children's literature. I have been searching for answers to the question: how do people in general, but young children in particular, develop a new language, and how do they acquire literacy in both first and second languages? On the one hand this topic embodies the universal phenomena of language acquisition, literacy development and children's stories; on the other hand it imbibes its ideas from certain contexts. I'll try to tell the story of both.

Since I was very young, indeed almost all my life, I have been actively involved in the peace and social justice movements in Israel. My professional life as a teacher-trainer and a consultant for language development has given me the chance to bridge the gap between some personal aspects and my political perspective. Dealing with languages is not purely linguistic. It is, rather, a subject that includes social-cultural-political aspects and, in areas of conflict like Israel, where I come from, those terms are expanded and become even more complicated. In the case of Israel these aspects affect both Arabic speakers learning Hebrew and English, and Hebrew speakers learning English and learning (or not learning) Arabic.

My research thus had two origins: one personal, and the other associated with my profession. At some time, these two aspects united to form a single entity and led me on a very special journey. In any case, these two worlds have constantly been associated with my socio-political involvement with the oppressed, and with an *intense* desire to write.

The personal aspect derives from my daughter and from what she has taught me, through her development, about languages. The following is how I described it in the introduction to my PhD thesis.

> My daughter was born in Israel, in a general-standard L1 Hebrew environment. When she was eight years old she taught me that the only thing that matters when someone wants to learn a new language is the meaning of what he/she learns, and its comprehension by and for that person. In fact, she taught me that twice. Once when she was eight, and then, again, two years later.
>
> As an eight-year old she used to watch a television programme that she liked very much. The programme had the same name as hers – Shera – and this was also the title of its theme song. As a Hebrew speaker she could not understand the English words of the song, but she could read the Hebrew subtitles; and as a child who was

attracted to music, she grasped the melody of that opening song and sang it – but in the Hebrew she read in the subtitles. One day I suggested that she should listen to the original English words and try to sing them in English. And, since she was already familiar with the meaning of the song, she had no problem in understanding the text and knowing what it was about. I guess that was her first start, her first 'affair' with languages in general and with English in particular.

The second time was two years later when she joined me on a visit to Boston. During the summer of 1996 I took some courses at Boston University, one of which dealt with literature-based reading in elementary schools. One of my tasks was to demonstrate reading a children's book to the colleagues on the course. Since I was interested in doing it in the most authentic way, I asked Shera (who was then 10 years old), and got her agreement, to join me for the presentation. I bought two books which I thought would be appropriate for her, considering her English proficiency, and asked her to read a page of her choice from either one of the books. I did this because I wanted to be sure that she understood the text.

When the time came, Shera joined me in class and sat beside me in the instructor's place, in front of the other students. The chosen book was on the table and, after I had explained the situation to the class, I started to read the story aloud, with no idea of what was going to happen, and what would develop from this situation. After I had read one page, to both 'audiences' – the students and my daughter – Shera asked me whether she could go on and read the rest aloud by herself ... and she did. Her reading was clear, relatively fluent, enjoyable and, above all, showed absolute comprehension of the text.

Thus, for those three weeks she was naturally exposed to and was able to look at various modalities of English – both spoken and written; and when we entered libraries or bookstores she was very interested in the shelves of children's literature. During this time we read several children's books together and talked about English and about literature. When talking about the books, she emphasised their contents. As she looked at and read the English language, she showed a general meta-linguistic awareness, transferring her knowledge of language in Hebrew to what she had just learnt in English.

All of this led me to deepen my inquiry, and convinced me to return to my earlier study on how languages develop, and the effect of literature on language development, and to examine these theories professionally.

* * *

Later, I wrote:

> Naturally, children are usually introduced to stories in their first language. Narrative text – both oral and written – seems to be the primary and basic text to which young children are exposed and which they use from their early years (Rigg and Allen, 1989; Meek, 1988/1997). This universal phenomenon is connected not only to cultural and social traditions, but also to cognitive and emotional aspects of the child's development (Smith, 1992). But if we assume that narrative is universal – then we can try to find out whether it could also be used in learning new languages. For it does seem that the means by which the brain absorbs, understands and imagines stories may also be transferred to another language, using authentic 'story language'.

For several years, I have worked as a consultant for language and literacy development and as a counsellor for Multilingual and Multicultural Education in the Basic Skills Department of the Israeli Ministry of Education. I have been involved in projects which promote cultural studies and bilingual education in and between schools and communities. Thus, within this framework, I have had opportunities for dialogue with teachers and students about theory and practice, and about ideas and concepts concerning development of language within a multicultural society. My initial idea was that through dealing with languages we could approach the whole range of social and cultural issues which could be so vital to the acquisition of new languages. It seemed then, as it seems today, that this linkage between languages and other issues is relevant to any learning of a new language; in the case of Israel the linkage is unique and even intensifies this notion. Bridging thus becomes sharing: language is the bridge; stories are what we share.

choice * writing * reading * questions * more questions *
some answers * children * literature * literacy * language(s) *
criticism * pedagogy * society * justice * truth * trust * teaching
* research * words(s) * world(s) * people * freedom

Following these concepts I began to wander from one school to another, meeting with a pupil, or a small group, or even an entire class, and reading them children's literature. I read books in Hebrew to Arabic speakers, in Arabic to Hebrew speakers – (though I needed some help from an Arabic teacher for that) and in English to both L1 Arabic and L1 Hebrew speakers[1]. The impact of those meetings and the reaction to them was splendid, and the results surprised me. Again and again students of different ages and different backgrounds identified and united with the stories and the new language from their varying points of view and from various aspects.

What was there in these stories that caused the students so to empathise and contract an alliance with them?

Dealing with languages is not just a linguistic issue. Dealing with languages through literature is not just dealing with literature. Dealing with languages through literature means entering the culture of a person or society, the spirit and mind of a person or community. It means communicating and relating to a person's needs by creating new insights that incorporate social values and literate understanding. In Israel, the context of languages includes issues of right and human rights, majority and minority cultures, identification and acceptance. It emphasises and raises acute questions concerning the status of languages, deepens the need to confront these issues, and encourages the hope that knowing the other's language helps to accept him or her as he/she is. All of this is connected to the belief that dealing with languages may bring new insights and understanding concerning the learner, not only of the new language, but also in regard to and as a retainer of her/his own language.

From this work a number of focal questions have arisen. This is how I formulated them:

- What is the role of literature in learning literacy in a new language?

- How can literature open doors to understanding new cultures? New languages?

- How can literature foster emotional links between children of different languages and cultures?

- Can children's literature function as a mediator between cultures and thus construct linguistics and socio-cultural insights?

- What is the influence of developing literacy in a new language on the literacy of the mother tongue?

As a higher education teacher I used to work with Bedouin teachers and trainees. From the very beginning of the course we discussed cultural and social issues in education. The core of the course was children's literature, used as a focus for examining the issues of developing new languages connected to personal and social attitudes. Seeing the enthusiasm of my daughter and the interest of my students, I decided to research the role of literacy in developing second languages, at different ages and in different communities, focusing on children's literature. This also gave me the opportunity to integrate and associate my political beliefs with the topic. In my work, I try to explore these questions in the socio-political cultural *context* of Israel, and to discuss their significance in the field of second language development in general.

Language

English is not my first language, yet I wrote my thesis, as well as my share in this book, in English. Though it is not always easy to write in a second language, and sometimes very difficult, it still has some advantages. Being able to write in more than one language allows me to express my ideas by reflecting my thoughts differently from using only one language. It gives me the ability to manoeuvre between the two languages, and to be more precise in both of them. From my experience, from my point of view, this empowers my writing and broadens my horizons both as a researcher and as a writer, and thus affects and enriches all my work. It lets me pause and ask: how would I say/write/express this in the other language? It is not merely a matter of finding the correct words (vocabulary), but also of structuring the sentences, and even the whole text. I don't remember being worried about writing in English. Indeed, I was quite excited about it. My feelings about writing in English as a second language, before beginning the project, became clearer as the writing continued. And I was not alone. There was Rena, who carefully read – and still does read – my work, and sensitively improved my written and hence also my spoken language. And, of course, there was Eve, to approve it.

I did not use my first language in the actual writing, and I certainly did not write in it and then translate my ideas into English. That would be like writing the same thing twice. But I manipulated, colluded, played with, the two languages when I took notes during talks, discussions, lectures or tutorial meetings, whether they were conducted in English or in my first language, Hebrew. I do the same with Hebrew and Arabic. In any case I viewed this ability as a strong point and so did the people who surrounded me. Thus, the multilateral process of writing occurs in my inner voices, in my personality, and is present in the dialogue between the languages I use. Writing is thus a very significant issue for me.

Writing

I define writing as a complex and changeable process of cognitive, emotional and social actions that takes place within and as a part of both the personal and the social system. It is a long-term, ongoing process of interrelationship between the writer and her/his facts, thoughts, feelings and insights. Writing is an infinite dialogue between the writer and her/himself, the writer and her/his topic and between the writer and her/his reader. This is how I developed my writing in my thesis. This is how I try to write my chapters in this book.

For many years I have been saying that, just as I like to read good writing, I like to read (and to hear) about writing, especially from the good writers themselves. I like to know about their writing activities, their thoughts and feelings about what and how they write. Thus for me, writing the story behind the big question means, among other things, writing about writing. It means writing about success and inner struggles, thoughts and feelings, about beliefs, criticism, and (special) needs, about good and bad writing, rules and the ability to break them, about problems and solutions, about books, influences, sharing, special moments and, above all, about hope.

Hope: changing reality. Following my research, I developed a *universal model for bilingual education* which has now been adopted in three new bilingual schools (Arabic-Hebrew) in Israel.

For me, this expresses our urge to fight for a better reality; sometimes to break rules. Naturally, this model will lead us to further big questions, to new researches and challenges.

* * *

The seal. Mahmoud Darwish, an exiled Palestinian poet, said in an interview:

> Hebrew was the first foreign language I learned when I was 10 or 12 years old. I spoke this language with the stranger, with the police, with the military officer, with my teacher, with my guard and with my lover. For me, Hebrew has no connotations with the language of the occupation, since I spoke words of love in it. This is also my friends' language. My attitude towards Hebrew is pure. It opened for me the door to European literature. I read Lorca in Hebrew... The Greek Tragedies I read first in Hebrew... This is also the memory language of my childhood. When I read in Hebrew, I remember the place.

Like Brecht, Darwish makes it simple. In the context of the Israeli-Palestinian conflict he manages, as one of the oppressed, to purify the language of the oppressor and to use literature as a bridge between people, cultures and communities.

* * *

So, if I want to sail I need that wind; but I also need to know what to do if there is no wind. I can dream about breaking the rules only if I know the rules; if I do not – I will stay where I am, and no wind can release me.

The wind may be our muse, our spirit, or our idea. The stick (pen/pencil) and the rag (paper) may be our word processor, our instrument. But then, probably all these combine with the internal fire, the intense desire to share these burning ideas, and tell their story to the whole world.

1 These were mainly picture books dealing with universal issues, e.g.
Brown Bear, Brown Bear, What Do You See? by Bill Martin, Jr. and Eric Carle
Cat on the Mat by Brian Wildsmith
My Best Friend by Pat Hutchins
Polar Bear, Polar Bear, What Do You Hear? By Bill Martin, Jr. and Eric Carle
Rosie's Walk by Pat Hutchins
Willy the Dreamer by Anthony Browne

Part two
Getting to work
The pilot study

Introduction:
an example of the problem
Eve Gregory

... individual comfort and discomfort become the only criteria for choice of social change and the basic contrast of logical typing between the member and the category is forgotten until new discomforts are (inevitably) created by the new state of affairs' (Bateson: 1979:222)

I n its widest sense, a pilot study allows you to dip your toe into the water without getting too wet. The pilot study is a practice run at analysing a small piece of data long before you need to tackle the main data collection and detailed methodology. Since it is a concise and well-structured piece, it gives the author confidence as a writer. So what is a pilot study exactly? I explain it simply as an illustration or an example providing evidence that your big question is, indeed, important and worth investigating. As the word suggests, a pilot study guides the reader towards what is to come. It also allows a pre-run with the methodology to be used. The evidence presented can be very small: a crucial incident or event from the classroom, home or community, a piece of spoken or written text or, more unusually, a string of past experiences from one particular context. Importantly, however, the pilot study should be able to stand independently and, as such, it provides excellent material for an early publication of the work.

What should the pilot study comprise? First, remember that the data presented needs both outer and inner layers of context within which it may be understood. The outer context might comprise an account of the area, its brief history and social make-up, a description of the school, community or classroom and its members as well as the customary activities within which the example sits. The inner context will move to the practice or event itself: how can this begin to be unpicked? Crucially, a pilot study should not serve to *answer* questions (otherwise there would be no point in continuing to the main study) but to raise further and more detailed questions arising from the data selected. By the end of this chapter, the author should feel confident in saying: here are my more detailed questions. The evidence presented shows that they are important and need investigating. Finally – and with the confidence that your questions do, indeed, remain unanswered – you can ask: how might these questions have been tackled in previous studies? This will neatly lead you into your trawl of studies for your literature review.

4

Only connect: making sense of classroom interactions

Jean Conteh

On being organised

The red notebook I bought proved to be too big, so after I had filled it I changed to using smaller, notebooks. I used these in many different ways in the course of my research, beginning by writing field notes on each visit to school in which I described the setting, what was happening, the people involved and reminders to myself of names and other details. I learned as I went along the importance of being as careful as I could about recording dates and times and so on; sometimes the significance was not clear to me at the time, but often became so later on. I also learned about spacing out my notes so that I could add other points later, if necessary. As I began to take a sharper focus in my observations – in the way that an ethnographic approach allows the researcher to do – I devised various ways of showing how something I noted on a particular day related to something which had happened earlier, or was something I needed to look out for in future.

My other purchase, the card index file, was just right; I now have three and will soon have to buy another one to hold the ever-increasing number of cards which record my reading. After a short while, I began keeping the bibliography electronically as well, but I simply use that one to cut and paste references from one piece of writing to another. I still depend on the cards to hold and carry with me to libraries or to stack together in sets when I am trying to construct an argument for something I am writing.

The importance of reading and writing

Students embarking on a PhD are usually aware of the importance of reading – there is the preliminary reading which helps to develop and shape the questions, then the literature review inevitably looms large. The writing can seem less urgent, perhaps because in some ways it appears almost too daunting to contemplate. There is a temptation to fall back on the apparent security of library searching and collecting references. But writing needs to begin early and speculatively; the notion of writing up as the final stage in research does not fit well in an ethnographic approach. The first piece of writing my supervisor asked me to do was an autobiographical piece. After several re-drafts, this eventually became the first chapter of the thesis. The power of autobiographical writing in many different ways became very clear to me when I carried out that first writing task. At the start of a PhD, it is an important means of reflecting on and understanding your research questions

Writing is a way of shaping and testing out emergent ideas and it needs to become part of the cumulative processes of selection and analysis through which the reading is sifted. It also aids reflection on the ever-growing body of data which fieldwork precipitates. Indeed, it is an essential part of the whole process; Gitlin *et al.* (1989:240) describe writing as 'the most pervasive fieldwork practice' and Ely *et al.* (1997:7) show how 'writing helps us compose and represent meaning from data'. Suggesting that it is valuable to see fieldwork, analysis of the data and writing as integrated processes rather than as sequential stages of the research, Woods (1996) argues that writing is part of the methodology. Fieldwork, analysis and writing all feed simultaneously into the weaving together of the strands which supports the 'unriddling' (Alasuutari, 1995:177).

Beginning the pilot study

After some initial talking, reading and writing, I needed to begin doing some fieldwork. My 'field' was to be a classroom, and I was certainly familiar with many of those. But I needed one where I was not familiar to the children and teachers who inhabited it, so that I could try to build up a relationship which circumvented as much as possible the teacher's or teacher-trainer's roles which were my accustomed professional ones. My other main criterion for choice was to find a classroom with children who had a range of different first languages, not so easy in Bradford where communities tend to be segregated and classrooms populated by children who share the same home language and cultural background. A colleague at college suggested I contact the headteacher of a small first school which seemed to offer possibilities. I did so and the head seemed interested. She asked me to put something down on paper which she could show her teachers.

This is what I eventually sent to the school. I cannot remember how I actually wrote this piece, but when I looked at it recently for the first time in more than eight years, it surprised me by its succinctness and confident tone:

A MODEST PROPOSAL FOR SOME CLASSROOM RESEARCH

I have been thinking for some time about trying to do some research into what helps children succeed in school, mainly at KS2.

At the moment, there is no funding (what's new?), but I have negotiated with the Language strand leader at college to have a bit of time to try to get something started. I would like to use the time (half a day a week, starting after Christmas) to come in to school and begin to get something together.

One aspect of children's school experience which I think is crucial in their developing effectiveness as learners is the extent to which they can negotiate the language (defined very widely) of learning situations. Classroom styles are clearly very important. I would like to look at the period when children have already established themselves in school, but are making some very important transitions (particularly in the Bradford context) – i.e. the years from 8-10, between first and middle school.

Ideally, I would like to spend most of my half day in a Year 3 class, following the children up to Year 4 next year and possibly on to middle school, if it all works out. The intention would be to get to know a small group of children and begin to develop a methodo- logy for investigating the kinds of questions I have in mind. They can perhaps be summed up in the one big question:

WHAT MAKES CHILDREN BECOME SUCCESSFUL LEARNERS?

While in the class, I would hope to be able to support the class teacher, and offer something back to the class in return for their hospitality.

The half day would be on a Thursday – I could probably negotiate morning or afternoon, depending on what would best suit the class, and what else is going on in college.

I would appreciate your initial response to this and, if appropriate, further discussion about how it could all be put into effect.

Thank you
Jean Conteh
B.I.C.C.
Nov. 13, 1995

About two months after giving the head teacher a copy of my modest proposal, I went to the school and met for the first time one of two teachers who worked on a job-share arrangement in a Year 3/4 vertically grouped class. The head had asked her and her co-teacher if they would like to take part in my project, and they probably felt obliged to say yes. Our first meeting, on the steps of a temporary classroom on a wet and windy January day, was rather tentative. Janet (not her real name) was probably wondering what additional burdens and responsibilities this stranger represented, and I was certainly feeling very unsure of my ground. The class had a singing lesson with a peripatetic music teacher after break, so Janet and I had a chance to sit down together and talk. I realised that Janet had not seen my original letter to the school and knew virtually nothing about my project, and that this was probably a good thing. This is how I recorded part of our first conversation in my field notes:

Janet was happy to sit and talk about how she tried to present things to the children; she said she was still trying to feel her way, after moving from Year1/2. She found that she needed to talk them through what was required – the children found it difficult to read through a worksheet or set of instructions and usually asked what they had to do. She said that she appreciated as much adult help as possible, as the children benefited from it a great deal.

I was extremely lucky in the way things worked out; Janet and her co-teacher Sandra, whom I met the following week, were both excellent teachers, highly committed to their work and to the children they taught. They also became very interested in my research and were very generous with the time and support they gave me. I visited their class about 50 times over the course of the next two years, accompanied them on school trips and local visits and interviewed them in the school holidays at my house. At the start, I tried hard not to present myself in any kind of expert role (though they knew I was a teacher-trainer, and at one point had a student from college in their class). It is clear, though, even from the short comment above, that from the first meeting the teachers perceived me as someone with professional knowledge who could perhaps help them in the classroom. This was probably an inevitable part of the way they viewed our relationship, though I would have preferred it not to be.

I agreed with Janet and Sandra that I would take field notes of what was going on in the class, and give them copies of the notes. What follows is part of the first set of notes which I gave to Sandra and Janet a couple of weeks later:

SECOND VISIT: TUESDAY, JAN. 30, 12.55 – 3.15

The school was broken into over the weekend and money had been taken from the office. The external door was boarded up. I asked about it in the staffroom, no-one seemed particularly bothered about it.

Sandra and Hazel were here; Susan was away on a course (which turned out to be the STA course at college). I didn't note times very carefully this afternoon, so this is an account of what happened.

Sandra had all the children (26) on the carpet to take the register. They were all quiet. One girl, Joanne, was moved because she was being disruptive. She obeyed, quietly. Some children were sent to tidy a table which hadn't been tidied before lunch. The children were talked through their tasks in quite some details; they all listened quietly to the whole set of instructions. My first impression was that Sandra's style was somewhat more directive than Janet's and her manner was slightly quieter. Each group was directed to its task:

Hexagons and Ovals: were to make 'mechanical monsters' from a story. Sandra told them that there were 'lots of things' they had to do before making their monsters; they had to prepare 'rough copies' of their ideas, then make a plan of their monster, a list of materials, etc.

Triangles: Taslim and Timi (Hungarian girl, who has just arrived with minimal English, in Year 4) making monsters with Hazel, other children playing a 'magnetic mouse' game

Circles: to work with Mrs. Wilson (not sure who she is) on games at 1.30 (big hand on 6), phonics sheets to do while waiting for Mrs. W. to come

Squares: to work with me on a science investigation (prepared earlier by Janet) testing the friction of different surfaces by rolling a car down a ramp

The concluding question, 'does everyone know what they're doing?' elicited the same response; 'ye-es!'

Science task with:	Becky	Year 3
	Darren	Year 4
	Anwar	Year 3
	Fozia	Year 3
	Parveen	Year 3

Testing how a car moves over different surfaces (worksheet prepared by Sandra). Children were not interested in reading the sheet, but keen to make sure they were doing what was expected. They understood the concept of fair test and recording ideas. They wrote words and lists fairly well, but balked at the idea of writing sentences. Darren very dominant, but in a positive way of wanting to get it done – at times, it became a little difficult to handle. The actual results were not of too great an interest to them, nor the discussion of conclusions, and what it might mean from a scientific point of view; they were eager to move on to the next thing. (Emily, who came up and showed me her new, warm jumper, noticed I had written two 'tos' in my notes)

When we had completed the activity and they had filled in their record sheets, some of the children went off to read with younger children in another classroom. I started to read a story I had in my bag 'The moon's revenge' to Parveen and Anwar. They went along with it a bit, but weren't too interested. Parveen asked if she could read her book to me (*Wonderdog?* from the Oxford Reading Tree) – she read very fluently and confidently.

About ten minutes later, the children who had gone to read with younger children came back. They talked about how funny the books the little ones had were; just a few words on a page. I pointed out that they had read this kind of books when they were younger, but this didn't seem to interest them at all.

These early notes were very general and descriptive, but also reflected my interpretations of events. Writing them up in this way was a somewhat onerous task. Indeed, I stopped doing it after a couple of months as it no longer seemed necessary; the teachers had stopped commenting on the notes very quickly, and did not discuss them at all after a few weeks, though I went on giving them copies. Our spoken – and mostly unrecorded – conversations about what was happening in the classroom, by contrast, went on throughout my visits. Sometimes, after leaving the school and anxious to remember something which had been said, I switched on the tape recorder while driving home and talked to myself in the car.

Despite the laborious nature of writing up the notes in those early stages, it was a very useful exercise. As I have already suggested, the writing was a valuable support to my thinking; it helped to familiarise me with the setting of the classroom and the players in this particular game of school. It helped to focus my thoughts and ideas, and clarify the aspects of the classroom context which it might be useful to concentrate on more closely. I continued throughout with the field notes. The children were curious about them, and often commented on them, asking what I was writing and wanting to make their own contributions, which I always allowed them to do. Other adults working in the classroom sometimes asked about them as well, and I provided copies for those who asked.

Moving on – collecting data and developing an analytical framework

At first, the teachers were reluctant to be audiotaped. It was about six months before I felt comfortable about asking permission to use the tape recorder in their classroom. By this time, I was feeling quite anxious because I had very little data related to the classroom talk, but – with hindsight – the delay and the opportunity, in Wolcott's (1975:113) words, to 'muddle about in the field' were positive factors. By the time I began to audiotape, I had been able to develop comfortable relationships with all the members of the classroom community, so I believe that no one found the tape recorder a threat. It was also possible to be quite specific and selective about the kinds of situation which I anticipated would provide the most appropriate data. This gradual focusing of the lens of observation was supported by background reading about the role of talk in the classroom, as well as the observations. My growing understanding of the relevant theories of language and learning was feeding into the methodological frameworks which I was evolving.

Almost imperceptibly, my research approaches had shifted quite considerably from my initial hunches about how to answer my questions. Here is an extract from my original research proposal, written *before* I began visiting the classroom, about what I thought I needed to do:

> During the second and third terms of Year 4, samples of general classroom talk will be collected, both from the classroom (classroom A) in which the children spend their time and, if possible, from a parallel class (classroom B) in the school in order to provide a context for comparison. The aim is to gather evidence of teachers' use of language (both spoken and written) over a range of situations, exemplifying the following discourse intentions, in order to establish the discourse climate of the classroom situations, i.e. patterns, rules, use of different languages, opportunities for negotiation, etc.
>
> – introducing topics
> – presenting information
> – setting and organising tasks for whole-class, groups and individuals
> – presenting cognitively demanding concepts
> – developing themes and concepts
> – summing-up and concluding topics

and children's responses in a similar range, e.g.

- answering teacher questions in a whole-class or group context
- in one-to-one interactions with the teacher (e.g. reading aloud, discussing work, less formal interactions, etc.)
- working with text in group situations
- presenting outcomes
- natural and spontaneous talk

This seems to lay out a clear and well worked-out plan. It indicates the need to collect samples of talk (and perhaps also of writing), related to quite specific classroom intentions and purposes, from the teachers and then from the children. It seems to be underpinned by a model of teaching and learning which is highly organised and even somewhat transmissive, and a view of success which is clearly defined and easily categorisable. The idea of collecting data from a second classroom introduces a possible comparative element, with the possible implication that one classroom can be labelled 'successful', and another 'less successful'.

As time went on, I realised that this approach was not what I needed at all. It would not capture the rich complexity of what was actually happening before my eyes in my chosen classroom. There were indeed rules, patterns, opportunities for negotiation and all the rest to be identified, but not in the way that my initial proposal seemed to suggest. I quickly abandoned any plan which involved comparing classrooms, teachers or children as I realised that it would be virtually impossible to control for variables or make any claims for comparability across any kind of sample, and I didn't want to do it anyway. Instead, I decided to identify and focus on a small group of children who could be presented as a case study of successful learners, without claiming that they were the only such children in the class, or that the class was more or less successful than any others. This fitted well with the ethnographic purpose of seeking to describe, and then to explain, but not to judge. The simple design also gave the scope to develop the recursive 'grounded theory' (Glaser and Strauss, 1967) approach to analysis which ethnography requires; the careful, detailed moving back and forth from raw data to transcripts to analysis and interpretation, and then back again to data.

The first hypothesis

In those first few months of classroom observation, what emerged for me as a significant factor for the children's learning was the quality of the teachers' talk. Because of their job share, Janet and Sandra often spent most of Wednesday afternoons together in the classroom. I had never had the opportunity before to be in a classroom with two teachers who talked to each other so much – which they did outside the class as well – and in such a collaborative way. After I had visited on a couple of Wednesdays (the exigencies of working at college meant that I had to abandon the plan of a regular weekly visit, and I visited as and when I could), I began to notice the distinctive ways in which the teachers conversed and included the children in their conversations. This is how I described these three-way conversations in my pilot study:

> As part of the arrangements for their job share, the teachers had a shared hour of liaison time on Wednesday afternoons. They used this time in the following way: Sandra was in charge of the class, Janet came to school and, with all the children on the carpet for about half of the hour, they had a three-way conversation about the work that had been done recently and their plans about what to do next. The children took an active part, answering questions and offering detail and comment about the work they had been doing since Janet was in school at the end of the previous week. They often provided information that she did not know, a somewhat unusual occurrence in most classrooms.

It seemed to me that the teachers and children together were, in Bruner's (1986:126) words, 'negotiating the world to create joint cultures', and at the same time the teachers were modelling for the children the ways in which talk could be used in the classroom to construct a joint culture of learning. I do not claim that this is an essential factor in all successful classrooms; models and definitions of success vary according to purpose and context. But I argued in my thesis that it was a very important element in the success of this particular classroom. Subsequently, I went further (Conteh, 2003) to suggest that the conclusions I drew in the thesis about teacher talk have important implications for teachers working in other classrooms, and for policy in a broader sense.

After six months or so, then, the first hypothesis to emerge from my classroom observations was that an analysis of the conversations between the two teachers would illuminate some of the ways in which learning was constructed in this classroom and success mediated. I asked the teachers if I could audiotape some of their Wednesday afternoon three-way conversations, and eventually taped twelve of them. These were the questions which the conversations raised for me:

1. What do the teachers see as important in classroom learning?

2. How do the teachers use language to interact with the children, to create a joint culture of learning?

3. To what extent does the language used by the children reflect that used by the teachers?

At the time, I was reading Courtney Cazden's (1988) elegant study of classroom discourse and saw clear parallels between the ways I was thinking about the teachers' conversations, and the ways in which Cazden analyses classroom talk. She identifies three main functional categories of *curriculum, control* and *personal identity,* and suggests that the 'the tripartite core of all categorisations of language functions' are:

■ validating and reinforcing subject knowledge

■ organising and managing different learning situations

■ making explicit the reasons for carrying out a particular task.

To me, the three-way conversations could be seen as achieving the following main objectives in terms of the children's learning, which are clearly related to Cazden's framework:

■ The communication of propositional information

■ The establishment and maintenance of social relationships

■ The expression of the speaker's identity and attitudes.

I distilled these objectives into three very basic questions, which helped me to understand the organisation of the teachers' conversations:

■ What are we learning?

■ How are we learning it?

■ Why are we learning it?

These questions represented my first attempt at developing a framework to analyse the purposes of the teachers' classroom conversations. But I also wanted to show the ways in which the teachers supported each other in their conversations, as it was their collaborative, intersubjective quality which had been so striking to me, and which I felt was important in the culture of this classroom. My problem was to find a model which would help to identify the social functions of the language as well as its organisation and none of the reading I did about classroom discourse seemed to go far enough in this direction.

At about this time, I went to an intercollegiate research seminar (Chris explains in Chapter Two how these began) where someone talked about conversation analysis and circulated a copy of part of a chapter by Drew (1990). I remember that there was a lot of discussion about how conversation analysis differed from discourse analysis. I went home from that seminar feeling very excited. Previously, my impression of conversation analysis had been that it was a highly complex analytical framework showing the subtle patterning of linguistic features in various types of conversation. Drew's model, with its sociological rather than linguistic lens, showed me another perspective; it offered scope to 'discover how participants understand and respond to one another' in conversations and reveal the 'intersubjective understandings' between speaker and listener. It seemed to be the link I needed between ethnography and linguistics to show how, through their talk, teachers and children were co-constructing cultures of learning in their classroom.

Reaching goals and moving on

I submitted my pilot study in January 1998. The main content was my autobiographical introduction and a detailed analysis of one three-way classroom conversation. I also included a section entitled 'Future Directions', which outlined the lines of enquiry I felt I needed to pursue. It had the following subheadings:

- Bilingualism

- Language, culture and schooling

- Models of knowledge in classrooms

- Children talking to each other

I had begun to see that my big problem could not be addressed by looking only within the confines of a classroom. I needed to explore the children's engagement with language in their homes and communities, as well as in school, to understand their viewpoints more clearly as well as those of the teachers, and the ways in which all of this was mediated within the political, economic and social systems that influence education in England.

After completing my pilot study, I submitted an article for publication to a refereed journal (Conteh, 2000), which focused on the teachers' conversations. Both the reviewers of the article and the examiner of my pilot study needed to judge my work by externally accepted academic standards. I found this daunting, but it is a necessary part of the progress towards PhD standard. Among many other – thankfully more positive – comments, the examiner noted the 'undeveloped theoretical/methodological' sections of the pilot study and made some useful suggestions for the directions which future work on these could go. The next task, clearly, was to begin work on the methodology chapter.

5

Drop the pilot

Chris Kearney

'Deep hanging out'

A pilot study is really a trial run. A way of testing out the big question, having a preliminary look at the material you've already collected and seeing what light that throws on your original intuitions. My original intention had been to use the interview with Aliki (not her real name) as a formal pilot study. But once I had got some way in I realised that it was not a proper pilot study, since I already knew pretty well what my main questions were and the direction of research. I also knew from Aliki's study and the responses I had so far that the methodological approach was likely to bear fruit. I have already mentioned the paradigmatic moments that came out of her interview in Chapter 2, but they do not amount to a detailed pilot study in the traditional sense. In the final analysis I included her story in the general analyses rather than either repeat it or indulge in an artificial separate analysis.

At a conference on the Ethnography of Education the organisers came up to me to talk about my paper. One said, 'But your work isn't really ethnographic is it?' I realised that he had a point. I certainly drew on a wide range of disciplines in my reading. But he was more concerned with my approach. I later realised that ethnography is a broad church and that he seemed to hold a fairly conservative position. I suspect one of the main reasons for his disquiet is that there appears to be no field and consequently no fieldwork. At least not in the traditional sense. My informants do not belong to one particular cultural group. I am not examining a particular site such as a school or a classroom. What I am examining are cultural processes, specifically cultural change. Moreover my reading has always been diverse and wildly eclectic; drawing upon numerous disciplines from cultural and literary theory to social psychology to unriddle my intellectual problems and dilemmas. Therefore it follows a different and less traditional path from Jean's study. It is closer to Aura's, but only in the sense that I felt it was all there from the beginning. There were two reasons why it departs from the norm.

Firstly, as the autobiographical section revealed, the genesis of the work was far back in the past and the questions tackled were ones I had been grappling with in my own eighteen year odyssey as a teacher; thirteen as a class teacher and five as an advisory teacher. This *is* my fieldwork. In educational ethnography we often undervalue our (often extensive) personal experience in multilingual and culturally diverse classrooms. Yet reflecting on it for this book I realise that it was similar to traditional anthropological fieldwork or 'deep hanging out' as Geertz puts it in his own autobiographical reflections. When I think back on my first teaching job in Hackney I can readily empathise with Geertz's declaration that:

> One of the psychological fringe benefits of anthropological research – at least I think it's a benefit – is that it teaches you how it feels to be thought of as a fool and used as an object, and how to endure it.

> Much more difficult to come to terms with, however, is another very closely related sort of collision between the way I typically see things and the way most of my informants do; more difficult, because it concerns not just the immediate content of the relationship between us but the broader meaning of that content, its symbolic overtones. (Geertz, 2000: 30-31)

These were the mysteries I was trying to penetrate and am still working on.

The second reason was that my thesis was going to be a refinement of questions I had explored in my MA dissertation. In other words, my MA dissertation *was* my pilot study. I will discuss this later in the chapter, but first I think it would be fruitful to look more closely at the genesis of those questions which emerged further back in my professional career. It will also contextualise it in current policy because my contemporaries and I lived through developments of policies that have gained prominence as 'equal opportunities' or latterly 'social inclusion'. In terms of my experience in schools there are several points where my attitudes and my own teaching changed significantly. I became aware of further levels of complexity. I want to map this journey.

Fieldwork becomes homework

Fieldwork becomes homework as differences between ethnographer and the subject under study are broken down as the ethnographer is incorporated into the text, and as theory and text reflect and participate in the multipositioning and fluctuating realities of quotidian life. (Lavie and Swedenburg, 1996:154)

I entered the teaching profession more by chance than intention. I had not harboured any long-term ambition. I had little experience of dealing with children. In fact when I left university I drifted in and out of several low paid jobs and ended up as a temporary clerical officer in the Civil Service. At that time it was a strange culture with arcane rules. The work was undemanding, yet stultifyingly boring. I found that by working quickly I could create some time for personal reading. One of the books I read in those stolen moments was *Summerhill* by AS Neill (1968). It came at the right time.

During my time at college I had been involved in what was broadly called the underground or counter culture. This had led me also to take a left wing political stance. My time at college was a political education and led me to read more accessible parts of political and sociological theory. My knowledge and interest in education in those days sprang out of a sense of injustice and a distaste for the snobbery and stuffiness of the establishment. Like many of my contemporaries I had an appetite for anything which I saw as liberating us from those old mores. In the early 1970s the whole notion of extending such freedoms to those who were even younger than ourselves was also attractive. It was the era of *The Little Red Schoolbook* and Ivan Illich's naïve views on deschooling society. The difference with Neill was that he was already doing it and had been for many years. Children did not have to go to lessons. There was a school council where the headteacher had exactly the same voting power as the youngest pupil. They made the rules together and had joint responsibility. It sounded radical and exciting. It made me interested in the whole area.

So I enrolled on a PGCE course. I realised pretty quickly that it was not at all like Neill had described and that 'being a private establishment' his school was not compelled to follow the same rules and did not belong to the same cultural traditions as state schools. In terms of my own political outlook there were contradictions. Neill's pupils came from relatively wealthy and privileged backgrounds. Although it was different from how I imagined it would be, by my final teaching practice I realised that I could do the job and I actually enjoyed working with the children. However, that final teaching practice in middle class Orpington in no way prepared me for my first post in the London Borough of Hackney.

The first school I worked in overlooked a large park. It was an imposing three storey Victorian edifice built in the late nineteenth century by the London County Council. It housed two quite separate schools. The ground floor contained the infant school. The top two floors housed the junior school, where I worked. When I started it was a large school with more than 500 children on roll. In my first few years I rarely taught a class with fewer than 35 children. In the playground were two prefabricated classrooms to take the overspill. In my first year I taught in one of the huts. The children were a lively group of eight year olds. They came from diverse cultural backgrounds. The majority of their families had come from the Caribbean, some from French-speaking islands. There were also children whose parents or grandparents had migrated from India, Pakistan, Bangladesh, Hong Kong, Mauritius and Cyprus. Nobody at that stage really understood the implications of this. Moreover, out of a staff of eighteen class teachers – in those days there were few support teachers – approximately fifteen of us were in our first few years of teaching. The teaching was very formal and the notion of equal opportunities did not have wide currency at any level. All children who were at the early stages of learning English or had reading, learning or behavioural difficulties were sent to the 'remedial' teacher. Instinctively I understood that the situation was unsatisfactory since there were many children who were bright and articulate in a streetwise way, yet they were not succeeding in the school's terms.

Another event alerted me to a deeper problem concerning those children we would now term bilingual. At the end of the year I had to prepare reports for parents on their children's progress. In those days there was not the same emphasis on assessment, recording and reporting as there is today. In my first year I was given a single red exercise book for my records, but no guidance on how to use it. When I came to write the reports at the end of the year I found I had only very sketchy information on two of the children in my class. They were both bilingual and both were girls. They had become in- visible to me. Neither had profound difficulties. Neither were high achievers in the classroom. They seemed to want to make them- selves unnoticeable. This made me very uncomfortable.

I had similar problems with the curriculum. There were very few materials or approaches which motivated the children. We also had a profound ignorance of what went on at home. What it meant to live within two cultures and speak two languages was a mystery to us. It was here that my fundamental questions were raised. If we were to provide an education where the children could achieve their full potential we needed to be more aware of what they brought from home. It is difficult at this distance to describe how few materials there were. The children's books which I loved and had used successfully in middle class Orpington, such as *The Silver Sword* and *The Secret Garden*, did not captivate the children. I dis- covered they responded much more readily to myths, legends and folk and fairy tales. Therefore I built up a wide-ranging repertoire in this area. I also built up an interest in storytelling since it is much easier to manage a lively class if you are looking them in the eye. We had many lively classes.

I also developed an interest in educational drama and found that this was a way of establishing a productive dialogue with the classes

I taught. Drama allowed us to explore a vast range of subjects and engage in making sense of the world. It gave me a deeper understanding of the children's lives, and it also raised a great many questions. I realised that the theory I was reading about multiculturalism and bilingualism did not quite coincide with my understanding of the children in front of me. By necessity such books contained generalisations and oversimplifications.

At this point in the late 1970s I enroled on a diploma course at Middlesex University and became more familiar with the theory of linguistic diversity. I was particularly interested in the relationship between language and power. This fed in to my growing understanding of the wider context and added several more layers of complexity. Moreover, through my work in schools, play-centres and youth clubs, I was engaging more fully with the life of the area. I developed a much wider taste in terms of music, art and literature. This experience was all the more powerful because I could engage with and appreciate it within a lived context. I am not pretending that I ever became fully immersed in that cultural life, but it deepened my own understanding and enabled me to have meaningful dialogues. I was moving from collision to collusion.

Shortly after completing the course, I moved jobs. I took up a post in Tottenham. Here the issue of multilingualism was far more prominent and obvious. A survey conducted by Haringey Council in 1989 demonstrated that 57 per cent of Haringey's population came from homes where English was not the first language. However, I felt that I was well supported. An advisory teacher came to work alongside me in the classroom. Through her own practice she demonstrated how monolingual teachers such as myself could support bilingual children in realistic and unpatronising ways. She also introduced me to a range of unfamiliar resources and some engaging theoretical reading. I also became involved in trialling the Open University pack, *Every Child's Language* (1985). Eventually I became an advisory teacher. Working as a member of the Reading and Language Development Team, I learned a great deal about the complex interrelationship between language development, literacy, narrative, power, culture and identity.

It was during this period that I enroled for the MA which was a pivotal event in my own development. It was here that I brought all of my interests together: bilingualism, culture, identity and narrative. From the outset, I was dismayed by the pre-eminence of failure in the existing literature on multilingualism and multiculturalism. I decided to examine how some children from different cultural heritages could, with sensitive teacher intervention, succeed at school. In the process I read a great deal of theoretical work in the area. Not only did this underpin my dissertation, it constituted the bedrock reading for my doctoral thesis. I knew which questions to ask and had a hypothesis of sorts.

I have spent a great deal of time on this section, but not merely to indulge myself. I wanted to show in a practical way that the fieldwork was already done in great depth long before I thought of a PhD at all. I really knew how I wanted to proceed. Two chapters from my MA dissertation had been published in refereed journals. This gave me a great deal of confidence in writing the thesis.

The MA as pilot
My account of this pilot is very brief, taking up a few pages in my thesis. Here I give something of its flavour:

> As much of the literature at the time seemed to concentrate on failure, both in terms of the school's inability to get to grips with issues of culture and identity and the well publicised problem of underachievement of ethnic minority pupils, I thought it might be beneficial to concentrate on success. This was the basis of my MA dissertation. In this endeavour I was fortunate enough to encounter Christos. He was a ten-year-old from a Greek Cypriot family. He proved to be a fluent bilingual who had strong links with his own community and a strong sense of cultural identity.
>
> Up until this point he had been thought of as a reluctant learner. However, as I worked with his class, he engaged deeply with the class project which was based around *The Odyssey*. An account of this was published in *English in Education* (Kearney, 1990:3-13) It shows how with some acknowledgement and validation of his own cultural traditions he was motivated to produce some exceptional work, both in English and Greek. This culminated in his production of a home-made model of a Greek library, which contained his re-

telling of the whole of the Odyssey in Greek. His retelling was presented on scrolls, which he had artificially aged by burning the sides. He had completed this at home in his own time with the help of his uncle. The episode demonstrated how much potential remains unfulfilled in many multilingual classrooms

It also highlighted the relationship between language, culture, identity and schooling. For my second case study I examined the case of Kofi, whose parents had been brought up in the Caribbean. He was also successful. But here I noticed significant differences from Christos. Whereas for Christos there was a certain congruence between 'where he was at' and 'where he was from' (to borrow Paul Gilroy's (1992) phrases), similar explanations did not work in Kofi's case. Instead I was confronted with more complex manifestations of identity. He appeared to have several layers to his sense of self and could draw on an array of linguistic and cultural resources.

Although the MA clarified many of the misconceptions I had held previously, I felt that I had only begun to investigate the mystery of what happens to people culturally and personally when they cross borders and particularly for generations who are born in the new place. These were the motivations for me to dig a little deeper.

On reading and writing

I maintained a holistic view of the research and tried to keep a keen eye on how the parts interconnected. I was very disciplined regarding the actual reading and writing. My course of study was part-time, therefore, like many students, I also had to juggle a demanding job (as coordinator of the primary PGCE course) and obligations at home. Although I would earmark particular days for more formal reading and writing, the less formal writing in my journal could occur almost anywhere and at any time. Moreover, I was always reading on my tube journey to and from work. It is always good to provide yourself with limitations. This is particularly true about the scope of the project. Resisting the temptations of working on a grand scale can focus the project and keep everything in perspective. My supervisor suggested that I should keep the number of people to interview small and manageable. As it happened, six relatively short interviews gave me more than enough material for the thesis. Transcribing the interviews still took considerable time. I would also tackle one chapter at a time to make the process manageable, working systematically through them. Very few were written out of sequence.

The importance when writing of audience and feedback

Having decided to limit my sample to six people I then had to decide where to find suitable people. Asif had been a student of mine whom I knew to be articulate and candid and Nandine I contacted through my supervisor. Once I had explained what I had in mind both expressed great interest in participating. I interviewed Asif and Nandine shortly after I had spoken to Aliki. This was useful since I could begin to see the pattern that connected them. Once this was done I presented my work in progress to three different audiences: the intercollegiate group, a group of teacher educators and students in Tampere, Finland and at the ATEE conference in Macereta, Italy. Presenting at the conference was far less daunting, having rehearsed the arguments among friends in the intercollegiate group. Responses were very positive and I made contact with others working in the area. Those dialogues continued and helped further my thinking. The discussions sharpened the writing, forcing me to be succinct and clear about my own ideas. It also forced me to select the most significant examples from the interview and begin to see patterns and identify areas to pursue further. Moreover, organising the ideas to a limited number of transparencies for these audiences gave me ready-made plans for the writing. An additional benefit, of course, is that an audience will ask you to clarify any points which are vague and ambiguous as well as making suggestions about ways of moving on, or suggestions for reading you may have missed.

The intercollegiate group were the first I discussed my work with. As Jean points out, we gained a great deal from listening to each other. Part of it was therapy since we were all at different stages and those further along the road always gave sound advice to the beginners. Presenting to that audience was the best thing for me. They were very supportive and constructively critical, really engaging with the work. Over the years they would also comment on the development of the ideas. It was usually after such presentations that I would submit a paper on that particular aspect to a national or international conference. This in turn would become an article for a journal. It would also serve as the first draft of a chapter of the thesis. Obviously these drafts would also be read and commented upon by my supervisor. So the same piece was used for a variety of purposes.

Establishing routines

My writing routine was regular and followed the same pattern. On my earmarked writing days I would get up early and begin work almost immediately, using my notebooks and my list. Margaret Meek used to tell us that all good writing starts with a list and that is how it is with me. My transparencies for the conference presentations often became the list. Talking about the writing process, the American poet, Gary Snyder says that sometimes the creeks are full and the poems flow; some days we heap stones. Isabel Allende describes the process as 'opening a door.' 'I go through the threshold and I enter a space that is dark, and inside is the story and my job is to show up in front of the computer every day and illuminate that space word by word until I get that story.' I guess most of us who write regularly can identify with those remarks. Unless we sit there and pound the keys, nothing gets done.

In the afternoons I would generally go into Senate House, the British Library or the Institute of Education library to chase up references and read around the area relevant to the particular chapter I was writing. I tried to keep it as focused as possible. In fine weather I would sit outside in cafes or parks and mull over the questions and ideas, noting anything at all that came to me in my journal. There were usually some nuggets mixed in with the nonsense. This kind of reading and reflection eventually grew into the literature chapter, but I didn't even see it as that at the time. The literature chapter took shape much later when I began to see that there was a pattern and a history to the development of the concept of identity in Western thought. In fact that search for underlying patterns is the way that the thesis evolved and took shape. It was what I was continually rehearsing and refining in my journals.

The interview with Aliki and the big question

The MA had led me to several conclusions; firstly that as teachers we needed to link more closely with what children from diverse cultural heritages brought to school. For this we needed a much clearer notion about those 'funds of knowledge', as Luis Moll calls them. Secondly we needed to explore the complexities which lay behind notions of identity. Thirdly we needed to examine successful students who could give us perspectives which could be used to extend this success to more pupils. Aliki volunteered to be interviewed after hearing me talk at her university. I prepared a list of questions which related to my own interests. I sent these to her in advance, but with the understanding that our conversation could be much more organic and freewheeling than a formal interview. We talked for about an hour and a half. A few days later I sent her a copy of the tape, asking her to let me know if there was anything there which was inaccurate or which was too sensitive to use. She said that I could use any part I wished.

Generally our conversation confirmed the complex and contradictory notions of identity I had explored in my MA. She said she felt that she had no real help from teachers and none had really understood and connected with what she brought from home in terms of language and culture. One anecdote she told became central to my work. When we were talking about her experience on her degree course in community arts she described a one-woman performance she did in her final year. It immediately seized my attention and I have used it on almost every occasion when I have spoken about my work. For me it encapsulates the dilemmas of crossing boundaries, which are cultural, political and psychological. Ultimately it led to my big question. Here it is:

– So school didn't help you at all, in any way?

No. No... I don't think... I had nice advice from college lecturers... I think the thing that really bumped up my confidence when I left drama school... We had a student initiated thing and I did a one woman show which was all about my culture. I'll have to give it to you... It's all about identity

– Tell me about it

– Okay....I'll tell you about it.

It's set in the future, in Cyprus. And the future is...that they've taken away the buffer zone, the green line, the separation line between north and south, between Turks and Greeks. They've taken that away and they've said to the whole country 'Do what you want!'. And the woman...this is the night before she has to go back to her village. Not [the one] she grew up in, because she was only a small child... She was seven when she left. Now she's in the south, with her uncle in the south, because her parents.... Her mother died and her father just disappeared.

And it's the night before [she is due to leave]. And the thing about Greeks is, that every single one of them will say, even the little kids, will say 'Yeah... One day we'll go back to our land,' And this girl has grown with that, from her uncle... And she's packing and, as she's packing, she's packing the things she's brought down with her from her own village, like her mother's apron. And she's remembering things about her parents. And as she's doing that she's kind of, like, realising... Because, it's twenty years later, and she's grown up and she's established herself down in the south. She's kind of thinking, 'Well? Do I really want to go back? And if I do go back, what will be there for me? That's old. That's past ....That was when I was a child. But I'm a woman now. And my parents are dead, (or they're not there any more). And if I do go back, what will there be there for me? The Turks have left the area more or less derelict, so I'm going to have to start again, and do I want to start again?'

She also has a relationship, at the time, with a British soldier. And they don't actually speak a language together. She doesn't understand English and he doesn't understand Greek. So their whole relationship revolves around: 'Yes' 'No' 'Yes' 'No'. Which is quite quirky! But they, somehow, manage to realise that they love each other. They understand those words. And the night that she leaves to go back to her village, because it is always assumed that she will go back, one day, he says to her, 'Let me take you to England.'

So, it's either a choice between going back to her village, where her ghosts [are], (and, that is past; that is history), or going with this Englishman to another country, which is foreign to her, that is alien to her, but she still loves him.....Does she love him? Or is it just a fantasy, a dream of being something else?... Or does she stay put, where she is; where she's grown up? [With] things that she knows; things she identifies with?

She decides to stay.

It underlined the complexities and intricacies of the human heart and how, often, the big decisions in people's lives are not the outcome of systematic and rational planning; not driven by career goals, but tucked away in small, secret desires which do not conform readily to the demands of power or at least not in obvious ways. I realised that if I was to fully understand the complexities of cultural change, I had to find a way of charting this process with my six participants.

Once I had completed my initial observations on the interview with Aliki, I was able to begin to articulate my big question or set of questions. Here is how it appears in the final draft of my thesis:

> My starting point was to find connections between success and teachers who were able to connect with their [pupils'] cultural background. However because the issues are more complex than I had initially thought, it led me to a more basic and complex set of questions which surround the nature of changing identities in modern cosmopolitan cities. In brief they are:
>
> ■ What are the changes in the notions of self identity and culture in educated second generation settlers in London?
>
> ■ What aspects remain the same?
>
> ■ What is the nature and reasons for those changes?
>
> Although there has been a great deal written on these questions in recent years in the areas of cultural studies, ethnography and social psychology, much of the literature remains abstract and speculative. On the other hand more detailed empirical studies tend to rely on concepts of identity which are limited and draw on simple and straightforward notions of identity. The few ethnographic studies which have been conducted have concentrated on single cultural groups. Those which deal with several groups have tended to be positivistic in approach. *As yet there is no systematic, phenomenological, cross-cultural study of adult self-narratives in the area.*

As for the questions, I pretty much had them from the outset.

Around Easter 1996, I scribbled the following questions in my notebook:

■ What is the persistence of cultural memory?
■ What are the tensions?
■ Is there a continuum?

- What effects change?
- Is it choice or necessity?
- How did those old currents, buried so deep, resurface after the collapse of Stalinist regimes?
- Why does a colonised culture persist?
- What is the phenomenon of syncretism?
- Is it just an overlay?
- Is it an interplay? A reworking?

Reading Frank O'Connor on the tube. What tugs at my heartstrings? What rings bells? How does it persist? What is the relationship between cultural memory, intimate media (family history, story, music etc) and the mass media? Is it levels of identity? Is it interplay and conflict? Is it a tension between intimacy and independence? The social and the individual?

Do you have to surrender your identity to be successful at school?

As raw as these observations are, they are the basic issues I grappled with. The methodology chapter helped me to clarify them, elaborate them, decipher some general patterns in the stories and discover analytical tools to capture the complexity of the syncretic process. It also helped me categorise and refine my reading. It clarified my own thoughts on wider concerns. This interlocking process ran on and on. It was a joy to live through.

On the other hand the last paragraph was written late in the day. By that time I was secure in my methodology. I had lived with this dimension of the research for several years. I'll admit that I didn't find it totally easy or straightforward. But equally I won't deny the feeling of joy and sense of deep play I derived from the process. As I've already said, Eve was keen that I begin quite early with the consideration of my methodology so that I would have a clear idea of the way in which I was going to approach the collection and analysis of our information. I am grateful to her for this since it is a complex concept, which I needed to get to grips with early on. I think that it was probably one of the most difficult parts of the process for me, but I knew I had to tackle it. And that's what happened next.

6

A journey through languages, literacies, cultures and children's books

Aura Mor-Sommerfeld

My work deals with the development of literacy in second languages. I have been searching for answers to the question of how people, especially young children, acquire a new language, how they develop literacy, what kind of relationships are formed between their first and second language, and what role children's literature plays in this process. 'What are your hunches?', 'Keep following your hunches' my supervisor told me again and again during our first meetings. My hunches were that literacy can support other language skills, and that children's literature can sustain them, since it connects with the knowledge that people have about books in general and texts and stories in particular. My aim was to investigate this, and to find out how literacy develops and what happens during the process.

In Chapter Three I described the philosophical context which is the infrastructure of my work and has textured my text. In this chapter I broaden and deepen the scope a little, beginning with a general outline of the socio-political and socio-linguistic contexts in Israel. I explain the Israeli educational system before discussing the language situation generally. This will help to give a better understanding of the later sections which discuss some aspects of my pilot study and the process of my research in depth.

Language and policy: Israel – a place of conflict

Israel is essentially a multilingual country with a multicultural society. Historical developments have created a unique and complicated situation in which two populations with two different languages live in the same state. There are the Israelis who speak Hebrew, though this language is not necessarily their mother tongue, and the Arab-Palestinian population, whose mother tongue is Arabic though most of them speak Hebrew. The creation of the state of Israel in 1948 has also created a paradoxical situation as regards languages. Hebrew is the language of the majority, but it is a minority language in the Middle East. At the same time, Arabic, the language of the minority population in Israel, is a majority language in the Middle East, and in some ways it is also accepted as a world language.

Hebrew, Arabic and English as means of communication

The main language for communication in Israel is Hebrew. Although Arabic was an important means of communication between Jews and Arabs during the British Mandate, this changed after the establishment of Israel. The Arab population, which remained in the new state as a minority, started to learn Hebrew. Arabic speakers recognised the need for Hebrew and the value of it for acquiring education and social and economic status in Israeli society. Arab members of Parliament make their speeches in Hebrew even though they are allowed to speak in Arabic, but the language of negotiation between Israeli and Arab leaders is English. Hebrew has become the language of communication between Arabic and Hebrew speakers in Israel.

The official status and the fact that a large minority of Arabic speakers live in Israel suggest that Israel could be a fertile soil for learning Arabic as second language, but the reality shows the opposite (Brosh, 1996). Encounters with Arabic are very limited for Hebrew speakers, there is not much sympathy towards this language and, as stated earlier, its value as a means of communication is very low for both internal and international needs.

The relationship with English in Israel began before English became the international language of the world and of the media. Road signs, signs on stores, computer keyboards, are all written both in Hebrew and English, but not necessarily in Arabic. English has a very high status in Israel and, though this attitude remains from the British Mandate, it is currently nourished by both English and American cultures and is true for both Arabic and Hebrew speakers. Nonetheless, it seems that up to now it is more important to learn Hebrew than English as an additional language for Arabic speakers living in Israel.

Hebrew and Arabic: some linguistic aspects

Both Hebrew and Arabic are Semitic languages. Although they come from the same family, they have two different styles of writing. They are both written from right to left, but the letters are different. Thus, for any Hebrew L1 or Arabic L1 speaker, learning all these languages – Arabic, Hebrew and English – means dealing with three different styles of writing.

Hebrew is a language which, over fifty years, has been adapted to modern needs (Bentahila, 1983). Its technical vocabulary has grown rapidly, and although it is a Semitic language there has been successful borrowing from European languages; the morphological problem which makes borrowing from European languages difficult has been resolved by transforming suffixes and prefixes into Hebrew.

The Arabic language is diglossic, consisting of the spoken dialect of each country – of which there are some 100 – and a standard written or literal-classical language. This means that different Arabic languages are spoken in different Arab countries – the languages spoken in Egypt, Jordan, Morocco or Israel are different from each other; it is even possible to find different dialects spoken in different regions of the same country. But any literate Arab can communicate with any other literate Arab, no matter where they come from.

The two varieties of Arabic used in Israel can, then, be said to stand in a diglossic relationship, each having a different function and status. Classical Arabic embodies the literary heritage whereas local Arabic is colloquial. Classical Arabic carries prestige, while local

Arabic is not socially valued in the same way, not only outside the country in which it is spoken, but also for the speakers themselves. Researchers (Ferguson, 1959, Bentahila, 1983) define classical Arabic as High and local spoken Arabic languages as Low. The spoken language is acquired as the first language, the language of the home, while classical Arabic is learned only in a formal educational context. Only classical Arabic has a written form – although it is possible to write the spoken language, the dialect. Thus, classical Arabic is used for literature, newspapers, broadcasting and religious ceremonies, while spoken language is employed for conversation and for orally transmitted folk literature. To use Bentahila's words citing Farayh, the colloquial may be described as 'the language of life' and the classical as 'the language of the book' (Bentahila, 1983, p. 5).

The education system in Israel
General description
The education system in Israel is basically public. There are very few private schools and all schools are under the control of the Ministry of Education. There are two separate systems – one for Arabic speakers and one for Hebrew speakers. To date, there have been only two successful attempts at creating bilingual schools in Israel, and a third school is now being discussed. These schools have adopted the universal model for cultural bilingualism (Mor-Sommerfeld, 2002) for their curriculum. Another school which defines itself as a *bi-national* school has been operating for about 25 years.

Studying second languages in Israel: policies and attitudes
All three languages – Hebrew, Arabic and English – are considered to be second/additional languages in Israel. On the one hand, the Israeli context provides a valuable setting and a favourable environment for acquiring these languages as second languages. On the other hand, however, the conflict which exists in this context creates a number of problems. Thus the educational system is not separate from the general social and political systems in Israel.

English is learnt as a second/new language by both populations of pupils. The English curricula are all aimed at Hebrew and Arabic speakers, though they are written more from the Jewish-Israeli angle and thus, in a way, they are easier for the Hebrew L1 speakers. The situation is different concerning Hebrew and Arabic as second languages. All Arabic L1 speakers study Hebrew as a second language. However, Arabic as a second language for Hebrew L1 speakers is a chosen subject, and is treated more as a foreign language than a second language, assigned only 2 hours a week whereas 4-5 hours per week is the norm for English. Hebrew L1 high-school pupils can choose other languages instead of Arabic and in addition to English, such as French, or Russian which is popular among children of Russian immigrants.

Hebrew as a second language

In Arab schools, students begin studying Hebrew as a second language in the 3rd grade 3-4 times a week at first, and later on 4-5 times a week. Some schools start teaching oral Hebrew in 2nd grade as a private policy. Since Hebrew is very important for acquiring higher education and social or economic status in the Israeli community, the attitude towards this language among Arab students is generally highly positive but, since the establishment of the state, it is impossible to generalise or speak of homogeneous terms, situations or attitudes concerning Hebrew. Considering the various factors influencing acquisition of a second language, most Arab students do much better in Hebrew than in other languages.

Arabic as a second language

The situation concerning Arabic as a second language for Hebrew students is a little vague, and there is a certain gap between the official or desired policy and the field. This gap stems, among other things, from the upheavals connected to the status of the Arabic language and from attitudes towards this language. For many years the concept about learning Arabic as a second language was that it is the language of the enemy and knowing this language for Hebrew speakers was connected to the need 'to know the enemy'. Very few scholars held the opposite view, i.e. the need 'to know their neighbour's language' (Mor, 1997), though during the last years this idea has spread and has become a manifesto of the Ministry of Education. Indeed, official documents recommend studying Arabic, and the beginning of the peace process between Israel and the Palestinians emphasises the importance of studying this language. In schools, however, nothing much has changed. In general, studying Arabic is not mandatory for Hebrew students and very few schools teach it. If they do, it is usually for no more than 1-2 hours a week. Only 6 per cent of all Hebrew L1 students take Arabic in the Israeli matriculation examinations (Brosh, 1996).

Another dilemma for scholars with regard to Arabic as a second language is the problem of having to learn both a spoken (colloquial) and a written (literary; classic) language. The diglossic nature of Arabic and the considerable gap between its two modalities give rise to basic problems concerning the methodology of teaching it. Unlike other language students, Arabic learners, both L1 and L2, must take the acquisition of two discrete linguistic systems, each with totally different textbooks and curricula (Brosh, 1996). Spoken Arabic is written in Hebrew letters, and the whole approach regards Arabic as a foreign rather than a second language in Israel.

English as a second language

Formally, both Hebrew and Arab schools start to teach English in 4th grade, but the field has its own rules. The tendency in most Hebrew schools is to start teaching English in 3rd grade, sometimes even earlier, with emphasis on oral language. Not many Arab schools begin English before 4th grade and in most cases this depends on when they start teaching Hebrew as a second language. As in Hebrew schools, they also start with the oral language.

English has high status and high priority in the Israeli educational system, and much effort is invested in reinforcing this language among the students. Access to English is easier for Hebrew students, as they are generally exposed to more English than Arab students. This can be seen clearly in the results of the state examinations. A question that should be asked regarding the development of English among Arab students is, perhaps more dramatically: How will a change of environment in general – books, computers, television – and using literature in particular as authentic text affect the Arab students' approaches and achievements in English?

A general note: foreign, second, additional or a new language?

The discussion regarding 'second' or 'foreign' is, to a great extent, relevant to the situation in Israel. As indicated before, it is closely connected to the status of Arabic among Hebrew speakers and the way Hebrew speakers grasp Arabic – as a second or a foreign language.

Back to the study

Some years ago I travelled about Israel in my professional capacity, carrying children's books in Hebrew, Arabic and English. In fact, this could be called a 'demonstration of use of children's literature in second language instruction'. My target audiences were teachers, school principals and inspectors, and the meetings were held in schools in different communities all over the country. During the lectures, I met children who were then invited to participate in demonstrating the use of children's books in learning a new language, and thus they became both colleagues and leaders throughout the project. During that time I could observe children meeting books in a new language. I read stories to and with them, recorded their talks and comments, and noted their reactions after they had read or listened to the books. Most of these meetings were one-off and none of them was extended.

The picture became clearer and clearer, and my questions seemed to receive more and more answers. The need to investigate this area deeply, and my intense desire to write about what I thought I had found certainly started me thinking in terms of a PhD thesis.

Finding a supervisor was just a matter of time.

'Everything is here/there'

'Everything *is* here', I told my supervisor when I first met her. I came with what I thought were fascinating data collected from young children, L1 Arabic and L1 Hebrew, learning in different schools and in very different communities. The data were about children's attitudes towards languages, mother tongue and others, their linguistic and metalinguisitic awareness, and about their knowledge of books in general (bibliographical knowledge) and written language in particular. There were also some fascinating items written by the children.

- Should we learn new languages?

- Which languages?

- If we talk about English and Arabic (for Hebrew L1 speakers), or English and Hebrew for (Arabic L1 speakers) – which would you prefer to study?

- With which language should we start?

These questions were addressed to two groups of 6-8 year old children, in two different schools, from two different communities: one of L1 Hebrew, and the other of L1 Arabic. The conversations took place in each class separately, and were conducted in the children's mother tongue.

What follows then is a part of the results, an example of L1 Hebrew children's attitudes towards other languages. We shall see the children's attitudes towards linguistic, socio-cultural and even political aspects. I consider these ideas as the basis for understanding so many aspects of my study.

So this is the story of my journey, which eventually became my pilot study. Its presentation is very similar to how it was presented in my thesis; except that, this time, it is interwoven with discussions – and there were many – I had with Eve, my supervisor. In parallel, I will show how I organised the children's answers into a coherent piece of writing.

This is how the first version looked:

- It is important to learn both English and Arabic; to know them to the same degree. English is an international language. As for Arabic, we need to learn this language in order to be closer to Arabs. In this way we can advance the peace process.

- We should study both languages. It is always good to know more and more languages.

- I think English, because this is an important language.

- I think Arabic, because we do not have enough contact with them.

- That is why we should learn more Arabic, so that we do have contact with them.

- English – because it is a widespread and common language.

- Arabic, because this is our neighbours' language, who live in villages around us. We should know how to talk to them.

- Arabic – why? English is a 'fast' language, it doesn't take long to study it. But Arabic is a slow language, it takes a long time to learn. So we should study more Arabic.

- Arabic is like Hebrew. It is not true that it is more difficult. If we had started it earlier we should have known Arabic very well too.

- English is more difficult to know, because there are no 'sounds' in English (*the child probably means pointing, like the written Hebrew*). It is written according to letters. We should know three languages. Hebrew, because this is the language we speak; Arabic – in order to make contact with people we meet, especially with kids; and English – because this is the world language.

- It is most important to learn English. It is important to learn English because all countries use it, for example on signs.

- It is important to learn English. This is an international language.

- Both. It is good to know English because sometimes we do not read subtitles fast enough, so it would be better if we could understand what we hear; and Arabic because this is an important language in Israel. Also, members of our government speak Arabic and it is important for us to understand them (*the child probably means that some members of the Knesset – the Israeli Parliament – are Arabic speakers*) and to be able to speak with people we meet in the street. In order to talk to them we need to understand their language.

This was, and still is, a wonderful piece; but something was missing. It looked like a chunk of words or sentences, and required a professional insight into the writing process. It required a new order which would demonstrate the variety of aspects that have arisen from the children's talk. The new version is as follows –

The idea of talking about languages was welcomed by the children. Some of them emphasised English as their favourite language, on account of its global use:

– It is most important to learn English. It is important to learn English because all countries use it, for example in signs

– It is important to learn English. This is an international language.

– I think English, because this is an important language.

– English – because it is a widespread and common language.

Other children voted for Arabic. This group demonstrated both linguistic knowledge and socio-political views:

– Arabic, because this is our neighbours' language. They live in villages around us. We should know how to talk to them.

– Arabic – why? English is a 'fast' language, it doesn't take long to study it. But Arabic is a slow language, it takes a long time to learn. So we should study more Arabic.

– Arabic is like Hebrew. It is not true that it is more difficult. If we had started earlier we would have known Arabic very well too.

One child said: I think Arabic, because we do not have enough contact with them.

His classmate responded: That is why we should learn more Arabic, so that we *do* (*the child's emphasis*) have contact with them.

A third group thought it would be right and necessary to study both. Here, the children showed their affection for languages, demonstrated some linguistic knowledge and referred to the political situation in the region.

– Both. It is good to know English because sometimes we do not read subtitles fast enough, so it would be better if we could understand what we hear; and Arabic because this is an important language in Israel. Also, members of our government speak Arabic (*the child probably means that members of the Knesset – the Israeli Parliament – are Arabic speakers*) and it is important for us to understand them, and to be able to speak with people we meet in the street. In order to talk to them we need to understand their language.

– It is important to learn both English and Arabic; to know them to the same degree. English is an international language. As for Arabic, we need to learn this language in order to be closer to Arabs. In this way we can advance the peace process.

– We should study both languages. It is always good to know more and more languages.

One child also referred to his first language, Hebrew:

– English is more difficult to know, because there are no 'sounds' in English (*the child probably means pointing, like the Hebrew vowel marks*). It is written according to letters. We should know three languages. Hebrew, because this is the language we speak; Arabic – in order to make contact with people we meet, especially with kids; and English – because this is the world language.

The second version looked much better. Everything was still there, but much more organised.

As noted above, I also collected data from Arabic L1 children (again 6-8 years old) and the same process was followed with the L1 Arabic speakers. In both cases I was impressed not just by the children's attitude towards English and Arabic (or English and Hebrew), but also by how they discussed the issue. They were not satisfied with their own statements about languages. One of the most important things in this discussion was their ability to refer to each other's opinions and attitude. Let me just show how the Arabic L1 referred to English vs. Hebrew. The children here seemed to have a more practical attitude, and their attitude to English seemed to reflect their dreams:

– For me it is more important to study English. Once I met a child and I could not communicate with him. Therefore I should study English.

– It is better to study English because we already know Hebrew. And since it is easier to learn Hebrew, it is better to concentrate on English.

– I think we should learn English. If we travel and can't talk English, we will not enjoy the trip.

- English is a beautiful language. We watch television, so we should study English in order to understand the movies.

- When I grow up I want to study medicine abroad. So if we start studying English now, I will know it very well when I need it.

I think that all of this sharpened the questions I already had but also raised some more:

- How do such young children present these ideas, perhaps even before they understand them?

- Where do the ideas come from?

- How do they take shape?

- What can be learned from comparing L1 Arabic and L1 Hebrew speakers regarding attitudes to other languages?

- How do the children develop their own insight?

- In respect of my study, could they reach a clearer understanding, different attitudes, through literature?

I wrote:

> Let us consider the theories about the world (attitudes) and about words (languages) that were combined in the children's responses. They require careful study in order to understand their meaning and to extend the interpretation.

But there was more – much more.

The bonus – a discovery

My interest in literacy in general, and in literacy development in particular, made me look very carefully at the children's writings that I had collected. I felt that I had something very special which I both *wanted* and *needed* to share with other people. Naturally, Eve was among the first.

The examples came from a variety of sources, but they all displayed the unique process of writing in a second language by relying on the first, while using two different scripts. This was a revelation to me.

Example one:

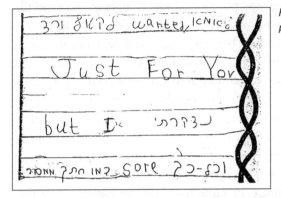

Figure 1 (3rd grade pupil, 8 years old)

This example shows transference from one language to another in a written text, using two scripts. The child's story uses Hebrew and English. In the last line he created a rhyme with the word '*sore*' and the Hebrew word (מסור masor): 'I wanted to pick a rose just for you. But I was pricked and it was so sore, like a cut of a saw (*masor*).'

Example two:

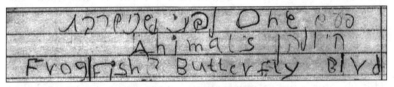

Figure 2 (2nd grade pupil, Hebrew L1, 7 years old)

Figure 2 shows the beginning of a story. It says: 'Once upon a time there lived animals: a frog, a fish, a butterfly, a bird'.

Initially one might see these efforts as games invented by children who are discovering new situations or new opportunities. I assume that they represent procedures adopted by children developing a new language. Does this mean that written interlanguage, or 'language mosaic', as I refer to it, is a necessary step towards mastering languages? Is it a new aspect of this discussion, and is there any benefit to be gained from such discussions at all? Does it enable us to discuss not just the new language, but also the mother tongue of the learner? And is there any possibility that literacy in a second language might facilitate literacy in a first language? My thesis discusses these questions.

All the while, I was reading about how literacy is developed, both in first and second language, but I found not a single reference to the phenomenon displayed above, namely how children mix their writing when they learn a new language, especially when dealing with different scripts. For me, the revelation was so powerful and meaningful, so visual, so extraordinary and universal that it swept me away both emotionally and cognitively. I felt that this was my bonus, that this was something that I *had* to investigate. I read Goodman (1990) and Smith (1988, 1992), Wells (1986) and Meek (1991), Gregory (1996) Bialystok (1996) and many others, but none of them referred to what I later chose to define as 'language mosaic'. In any case, it promptly directed me to the next step – reviewing theories and examining how the existing literature on second language and on developing literacy in first and additional languages relates to my topic, and in particular to my questions.

'Everything is there, you see, everything is there', I kept saying, not just to Eve but to anyone who would listen. I am still collecting examples, and I have extended my search. I now know much more about 'everything', and it still attracts and fascinates me, makes me excited. In Chapter Nine I discuss the methodology I used to analyse and understand it all better.

A final note

This chapter is not so much about how to set up a pilot study but about how to develop one; I propose a doing-writing symbiosis. As Jean notes in Chapter Four, 'writing needs to begin early and speculatively; the notion of 'writing up' as the final stage in research does not fit well in an ethnographic approach'. A research study is an ongoing process of reading and writing, of dialogue between the writer and her/his study. It is obvious that at some point the researcher will emphasise a specific aspect, but from my experience I can state unequivocally that reading and writing, talking and discussion will continue until a work is completed.

The closing paragraph of the introduction to the pilot study finally read as follows

> There are four sections in the chapter. The first section presents children's *attitudes towards new (and other) languages* and their

discussions about languages. The second raises the issue of *linguistic and metalingusitic awareness* among young children in regard to new languages. The third section discusses children's *bibliographical knowledge* and their *concepts about print*; and the fourth illustrates *new paths to writing* through '*language mosaic' features*, suggesting a new view on how young children develop writing in L2. Thus, by setting the context, each section presents episodes, highlights questions underlying the research, and illuminates the ideas of the whole study.

This was how I finally organised the work.

Note

1   All participants' names have been changed.

Part three
the turning point:
methodology

Introduction:
taking decisions

Eve Gregory

> Science sometimes improves hypotheses and sometimes dis-
> proves them. But proof would be another matter and perhaps
> never occurs except in the realms of totally abstract tautology... let
> us say that truth would mean a precise correspondence between
> our description and what we describe or between our total network
> of abstractions and deductions and some total understanding of
> the outside world. Truth in this sense is not attainable. (Bateson,
> 1979: 27)

The methodology chapter in an ethnographic study is a
powerful statement, not of any abstract truth, but of the
author's political beliefs. In Chris's words: 'Your methodology
is *your* philosophy of truth. If you don't recognise that, then you
can't really go on. Perhaps, crucially, the difference between
'method' and 'methodology' is that the methodology is the philosophy, it's the politics...' It is here that your obligation to your participants is tested and the ways in which you collude with them to
reveal their stories and their interpretation of events. This obligation is not only to your participants but also to yourself as author.
The methodology chapter is the turning point where the work
suddenly becomes your own; it is about unique ways of dealing
with unique data. Until this chapter is written you usually find that
you have so much data and so many different paths to go down – in
Jean's words, it is like 'being in the woods, but I couldn't identify
where the trees were.' The methodology chapter is about deciding

on one or two particular paths through the woods from the many opening up, about making choices on what to include, how to include it and, above all, what to leave out. Your methodology provides you with a route through the jungle of data. For this reason, it is important to tackle it before you begin any main data analysis.

It is true that for many, including all the authors of this book, this is the most difficult chapter in the study to write. I suggest that this has nothing to do with its structure or content but has to do with how best to stay loyal to your participants and tell their story as you think it should be told. It is also true that, for many, writing this chapter involves a process of transformation. In Aura's words, 'you enter the chapter struggling to find your way; you emerge at the end confident and clear, having finally taken ownership of the work'. When written, the chapter provides a huge step forward quite disproportionate to the length of the piece. To continue the earlier analogy of paths through woods and jungles, completing the methodology chapter means turning the corner and suddenly seeing through to the clearing ahead.

But, practically, what might this chapter comprise? Briefly, the chapter might have two or possibly three sections. The first addresses general questions such as the following: What other approaches have been used to investigate and analyse areas similar to my own? Why will those approaches not suffice for me? What is ethnography and how is it distinguished from other research approaches? Why is this the best approach for me? What specific ethnographic methods do I use? How do I situate myself in the research? What are the drawbacks in ethnography for answering my questions? Do I need additional approaches? If so, what and why? Finally, what ethical issues dominate my work and how do I deal with them?

A second section might usefully extract one or more small pieces of data from the study and actually unpick them using the methods outlined above. This makes your methodology absolutely clear to your readers and furthers the trustworthiness of your work.

Finally, your chapter may go on to outline in detail the design of your study. Sometimes, this is best placed in a separate chapter; the determining factor being length. This is a meaty chapter and you should be aware of this before starting on this crucial part of your work.

To finish, three principles to consider as you write:

- Do be honest about your problems and even your mistakes. Let readers know what you might do differently another time

- Do be open about your own role in the research. Remember, ethnography recognises the role of the researcher both in changing events and changing yourself

- Do be meticulous in your presentation of detail. This is important for the trustworthiness of your work.

In the following three chapters, Jean, Chris and Aura disclose their own unique ways of tackling the hardest part of the work.

7

Going round in circles: developing the methodology

Jean Conteh

Taking an ethnographic approach

As Eve has pointed out, ethnographic research begins not with specific, detailed questions but with an overall big question or problem. When I re-read my pilot study recently about six years after I had written it, I was struck by its focus on what I had seen and heard in the classroom and my attempts at interpreting it. References to methodology were very sketchy. Eighteen months after beginning the project, I still seemed to be trying to identify what for me the problem actually was in the situation in which I had chosen to work. I can see now that this concern with working out my own viewpoints on the situation, besides defining the problem, was actually a vital part of developing the methodology. Wolcott (1975) suggests four 'criteria for an ethnographic approach' to research in schools:

- the appropriateness of the problem
- the appropriateness of the ethnographer
- the appropriateness of the research climate
- the appropriateness of expectations for the outcomes of the study.

These criteria are embedded and permeable layers of the same entity, each in dialogue with the others. They are the what, who, how and why elements of the project. One cannot be understood in isolation from the others, and none can make sense without recognising the self (indeed, the different selves) of the researcher who is at the centre of them all. The what, the how, the why and, indeed, the who are all constructs, aspects of the researcher's interpretation of the problem, a reflection of her own identity in the project. In intuitive and possibly unspoken ways, interpretation begins as soon as you open your eyes and ears to the situation which is the context for your research. Someone else who looked at the same situation could see a different problem, construct different questions and find a different point from which to start.

I began to see that, for me, the what and the why were very closely connected, even – perhaps – the same thing. When I look back at my early writing about the children in their classrooms, my descriptions of what I see and hear are always linked with speculation about what needs to be done. Here is a paragraph from something I wrote in 1996; I think it was part of an early draft of the autobiographical piece which eventually became Chapter One of the thesis:

> ... the more time I spend with children of 8 or 9 years old, the more impressed I am by their original thinking, energy and awareness of language, particularly bilingual children, who will often make the most interesting and perceptive comments about what they have heard and read. So much of this seems to be curtailed in the process of their schooling. It does not count because it is not recognised as representing achievement in terms of the National Curriculum. It is almost as if there is a whole parallel education system coming into existence. Children's minds will continue to grow and develop, despite the judgements that are made of their ability. The problem is that the more accepted notions of achievement fail to recognise how real children actually do learn, the more the growth and development is subverted. At a national level, standards may continue to fall, not because children are becoming stupider but because the real learning is not taken into account. This is highly dangerous, both for the individual learners concerned, who are faced with the label of failure, and for society as a whole, where so much potential is wasted, or – worse – subverted into negative effects.

While I may feel slightly embarrassed at the messianic tone of the writing, I make no apology for it. I felt passionately about the injustices I perceived in what was happening to the children in the classrooms. I realised that if I was going to do research into the issues, I needed to take my own feelings into account. I think the paragraph clearly expresses how, for me, carrying out this research was partly motivated by seeking to right the wrongs inflicted on the children by the system. My ethnographer's self had to include a political dimension and I needed to make that clear from the start.

One of the key goals of ethnographic research, for me, is to make a contribution to ongoing social change, albeit in slow and incremental ways. This may not be direct action such as reform of educational policy or practice, but may be more about revealing the evidence which challenges normalised viewpoints, values and attitudes. This helps to make sense of Hymes' (1981) statement that ethnography is the methodological approach 'most compatible with a democratic way of life'; an assertion which surprised me when I first read it.

As time went on, I came to recognise its implications for my own research. As Hymes suggests, ethnography offers opportunities to analyse ways in which knowledge can be controlled by the 'experts' at the expense of the powerless. The understanding gained ought to be empowering to the community being researched and not just to the individual researcher. Cameron *et al.* (1992) write about how 'empowering research' is research 'on, for and with' the community being researched.

When I started my project, I believed I had to do research on and for the children, their teachers and their families. It was only much later that I came to recognise that perhaps I ought to be doing it *with* them as well – and this has implications for the kinds of action which the research can lead to.

Methodology, then, is much more than the set of methods that are chosen to answer the research questions, more than a list of ways of doing things or a set of tools for collecting data. Your methodology is, in effect, a reflection of yourself and your values, the product of your decisions about how to act in a particular social and cultural situation in which you have identified a problem, a belief that doing something in that situation is better than doing nothing. The action you take may be entirely to do with the development of your own knowledge and understanding or it may include social and even political outcomes. As you proceed, you have to learn to live with doubt and uncertainty and – always at the back of your mind – the lurking suspicion that you might be totally wrong.

Strands of the enquiry – reading and writing

Reading and writing are woven into the fabric of the fieldwork of ethnographic research. The ways in which we use the word ethnography reflect this – we talk about doing ethnography and also about writing ethnography. The product of the writing can be called an ethnography, which others may read. It is not the same with questionnaires, interviews or other such research methods.

In doing the work of developing the methodology, one of the hardest things I found was to keep things moving on many different fronts at the same time. There was a lot to do; the children I was studying were moving on to middle school and I needed to visit their classrooms and talk to their teachers, then visit their homes again to talk to their parents. There was an ever-growing pile of tapes to transcribe. I had a long list of references to follow up. I also had a day job to do, and family responsibilities. At times, I did not know in which direction to turn next. This uncertainty is an inevitable part of the emergent, contingent nature of ethnographic research, but it does not make for a peaceful life.

Eve's advice after the pilot study, as ever timely and perceptive, was to think of titles for the different chapters I anticipated including in the final thesis. I did this, and added short explanatory paragraphs about what the content of each chapter might be. I subsequently kept on adding to this switching things around as new ideas emerged and the links between sections became clear to me. I kept this file on my computer entitled 'plan' and reworked it constantly. Towards the end, I renamed it 'contents', and reformatted it to become the *Table of Contents* for the finished thesis.

My reading ranged widely, largely guided by following up references and suggestions from fellow researchers from one article or book to the next, not by doing library-based key word or internet searches.

Some texts I studied closely, others I skimmed and scanned. A few texts I read several times over at different stages of the project, lending a recursiveness to the reading which matched the development of my theoretical viewpoints through the progress of the research. This reading and rereading helped me construct my own definitions of key words and themes and link ideas in my own way.

One important text in the early stages was Edwards and Mercer's (1987) lucid account of interaction between teachers and learners in the construction of *Common Knowledge*. At the time I was doing the pilot study, it was very influential in my thinking about classroom talk, particularly in the ways in which it conceptualised ideas of context, continuity and knowledge as a social construction. I used it extensively in analysing the teacher-talk which I discussed in Chapter Two of the thesis. When I began to consider issues about culture and learning, I read it again. It took me a while to realise that, in their references to culture, Edwards and Mercer had different meanings from mine. When they wrote statements such as:

> What we need is an understanding of education as a process in which children are helped and guided into an active, creative participation in their culture. (1987: 36)

they raised a lot of questions for me. I wondered about the use of the word *their*, preceding the word *culture*. I wondered whose culture Edwards and Mercer were talking about here. Were they saying that education needed to be no more than guiding children *into* a culture, whoever owns it? Were they also recognising that education should be about engaging dialogically with what children bring to classrooms, in order to help them to learn with self-confidence and power? I realised that my own developing theory of culture in classrooms needed to go beyond that which Edwards and Mercer seemed to be advocating, to include things which happened outside classrooms as well, i.e. I needed a much stronger notion of context.

I turned to references, largely from the USA, which problematised issues of teaching and learning in mainstream schools for children from minority ethnic, language and cultural backgrounds. The studies which appealed were those which captured what Ogbu (1981:21) called 'the texture of life' and made the children (and their teachers) real for me – perhaps they resonated with my 'experiential, embodied knowledge' as Shirley Brice Heath suggests (see page 8).

I remember, for example, reading Rists's (1970) sociological study of teacher expectation in a so-called 'ghetto' school, where he showed me powerfully and painfully, as Edwards and Mercer had not, the ways in which children engage actively in the construction of cultures in the classroom, at times despite and not because of the teacher's support. I almost wept when I first read Rist's descriptions of the injustices meted out to the children on 'table 3' in the kindergarten that was the site for his study. In effect, they taught each other from the bits of talk they overheard the teacher directing at table 1, where the 'able' children sat.

There were many more studies like this. Trueba's (1989:36-40) arguments for the claim that many aspects of school failure are *culturally* and not *cognitively* based resonated strongly with my own emerging ideas – here was a way of thinking about culture which seemed to offer more potential than Edwards and Mercer. I began to list references to culture that appealed to me, and they were eventually written into a preface to the theoretical and methodological section of the thesis.

My research project started as a personal quest for justice for the bilingual children I had taught. I was encouraged in this quest by studies like Rists's and those reported by Trueba. I had an emerging theory of culture. I saw that, to make it relevant to education, it needed to be related to a theory of learning. I found this articulated by cultural psychologists like Cole (1985, 1996), whose writing about learning and development recognises the ways the individual and the social come together and 'culture and cognition create each other'. Cole showed me how these factors are significant to individual learners' differential access to the scaffolds available in any classroom and thus to their success. In this way, he helped me to recognise the political dimensions of Vygotsky's socio-constructivist model of learning and the ZPD.

The methodology was becoming ever more layered and complex. Piece by piece, I was constructing the analytic frameworks necessary for the interpretation of my data. But I began to worry that my original hunches about classroom language were getting lost in all the other layers which were developing around it, that – to twist the conventional metaphor – I was in the woods but was losing sight of the trees.

A big breakthrough, which came quite a while after I had completed the pilot study, was the discovery of Critical Discourse Analysis and the work of Fairclough (1989). Here was a framework which gave me the scope to analyse the discourses of the children's classrooms and homes in terms of the wider cultural and political structures which mediated their production and interpretation. It allowed me to analyse in detail short extracts from my data, situating them within the wider contexts I was exploring. Using ethnography and CDA together immediately felt as if it would have great potential.

Then I came across the writing of the Santa Barbara Discourse Group (1992a, 1992b, 1995), who had actually started to do this. Reading their richly detailed analyses of classroom interaction which showed how the local events of the classroom were influenced by wider social, cultural and political factors was like pulling Excalibur out of the stone. I had found the instrument with which to continue the quest.

Strands of the enquiry – talking and doing, and listening

Through briefly describing some of the things I actually did in carrying out the fieldwork – my methods, if you like – I want to show in this section how in ethnographic research the conventional criteria of objectivity, validity, reliability and generalisability need to be transformed into judgements about subjectivity, authenticity and trustworthiness. Issues of bias and neutrality are crucial in all research, but I very quickly realised that the obligation to eliminate bias is sterile – a far healthier approach, I discovered, was to recognise and try to account for all the biases, including my own, which the various participants brought to the research. Ethical judgements need to be embedded in the day-to-day activity of ethnographic research and not merely ticked off on a checklist or set of guidelines.

I found quite difficult, for example, the stipulation to anonymise data by using pseudonyms and so on. Who was I, arbitrarily to make such decisions on the part of my 'subjects'? Some of my participants told me quite firmly that they wanted their real names to be used in the thesis and in the book which I wrote afterwards. In the end, they agreed that I should change them as the confidentiality of other participants could have been betrayed if I had not done so. But everyone agreed with the decision to use the real name of the city in which the research took place. I believe that all the arguments I made about the importance of history and social context would have been compromised if I had not done so.

After reading what Chris wrote about transcribing in Chapter Eleven, I added listening as a strand of the fabric of the enquiry, along with talking and doing. Like him, I did all my own transcribing and – like him – recognised the value of having the voices of my interviewees resonating in my head as I tried to interpret them. They still resonate, whenever I read the transcripts again. This was part of the reason why I decided to try to capture the paralinguistic features of my interviewees' talk in my transcriptions and analysis of their meanings; the rise and fall of their voices, the places they paused and hesitated and where they speeded up, as if to distance themselves from what they were saying were powerful means of understanding their meanings.

I did not make a detailed research plan, but allowed events to unfold, following opportunities as they arose. This openness to contingency is, I believe, an important feature of ethnographic research. It meant I followed several false trails – for example, I collected quite a few samples of children's writing, which I could not think what to do with. And it also led to fruitful serendipity; at one stage, I was able to get away from college half an hour earlier for a few weeks, which meant that I could have lunch with the children, and the conversations we had at these times resulted in some of my richest data. At another time, when I was particularly busy, I was invited to go to Pakistan to take part in a conference. When I told Eve of this and of my worry about getting everything done, she suggested I look on the trip as part of the research. It proved an excellent opportunity for me to talk to teachers in Pakistan and also to reflect on some of my developing analyses of classroom talk.

The main methods I used were those of observation and interviews. I spent roughly 200 hours with one or some or all of the children together in different classrooms in a total of four different schools. I believe it is tautological to speak of participant observation. One of the most basic requirements in trying to develop an ethnographic approach is that the researcher recognises the ways in which she herself is present in the context, just as much a participant as everyone else, though obviously in different ways.

Indeed, one of the problems of observing in schools is that you have to take on a role. An adult cannot simply hang around in a classroom for very long – the risk, in current classroom climates, is that you stop being seen as an observer and are seen as an inspector. Many of the children asked me if that was what I was. I am sure that the teachers saw me in this way, too, despite my best efforts. But over the 18 months in which I was a visitor to the first school classroom, the two teachers, Janet and Sandra, and I got to know and trust each other. I tried to offer help in ways which I hoped would add something to the life of the class, but not be seen as judgemental. For example, when they were working on a National Curriculum topic about St. Lucia, I took in a collection of artefacts and books of Caribbean stories. When a reference to breadfruit puzzled the teachers as neither of them had ever seen one, I volunteered to get one in the market, then a group of children cooked it and the whole class were encouraged to taste.

As much as I could, I avoided getting into conversations with the teachers about the best ways of doing things, but we did get into professional discussions and I think I did influence their practice in small ways. We often sat and talked after the end of the school day, and they would ask me for my impressions of events that had happened in the course of the afternoon. I remember discussing at length the three-way conversations I describe in Chapter Four and I think this affirmed the teachers' perceptions of their own expertise. Once or twice afterwards, I overheard them say to each other, 'Let's have a three-way conversation.' They took a great interest in my observation notes and the analyses I showed them and sometimes added illuminating comments of their own. When Ofsted came to visit, the teachers asked me for copies of my transcripts and analyses of their science work, and placed them in their files for the inspectors to see.

And then there were the children. I worked to establish a slightly less teacherly relationship with them in the hope that this might lead to more open responses on their part – and so, I hoped, more data! At times, this conflicted with the responsibilities of my role, perceived by the teachers – and, indeed, by the children – as a helper. I am sure it disrupted, at times, the children's perceptions of how adults should behave in classrooms and so it risked chaos. I dreaded being left in charge of the children, as it meant I had overtly to become a teacher while I was spending the rest of the time pretending I wasn't one. Another complication arose as I got to know the group of four children who became the focus of the study and visited their homes. They began to regard themselves as 'my' group and would sometimes use this dubious honour to claim personal kudos over the other children, at times taking liberties with my already shaky authority.

As the children moved into Year 5 in middle school, things changed. I arranged to visit the two different schools they were moving on to and asked if I could observe in their classes. The teachers involved all willingly assented to my presence in their classrooms, and several were interested in discussing their work with me. I tried to avoid saying too much about the research, presenting it not as a study of classroom interaction, but more as a monitoring of the children's progress, which – at this stage – it was becoming as I had lost the opportunities for closely-focused observation of one particular context. Instead, I observed a wide range of subjects and several different teachers. Most of the time, it was one class taught by different teachers and occasionally, it was one teacher working with different classes of children. With permission, I took field notes and recordings in all the classroom settings.

All this meant that I did not form the same close relationships with any of the teachers as I had done with Janet and Sandra in the first school. The relationship with the children, also, was changing. On the days I appeared in the middle schools, they were always very happy to see me. They no longer thought of me as a somewhat defective teacher; I ate lunch with them and chatted with them at breaktimes. Our conversations began to include more personal concerns. They always asked after my own children, and remembered the various things they had been doing over the years.

When it got to time to prepare for SATs in Year 6, the girls came to my house to practise some Maths and English questions.

Along with all the sitting around in classrooms, I conducted interviews. 'Conducted' sounds too formal for what I really did, and I even find it difficult to say specifically how many interviews I carried out. What I actually did was have as many conversations as I could with the parents and teachers of the four children. When I say parents I actually mean mothers, elder sisters, aunts and, in one case, an uncle. I was introduced to three of the fathers – I never met the fourth – who wanted reassurance that what I was doing would be helpful to their children. Then they went about their own business, leaving me with the women.

I visited all the homes at least three times, and one several times more. I always thoroughly enjoyed these visits, apart from the one or two occasions when I was parked in the front room with a cup of tea and piece of cake on the best china to wait while everyone withdrew to conduct lengthy family business in adjoining rooms. Usually, I sat in the kitchen and talked with whoever came and went, enjoying the generous hospitality and warmth of close and supportive family settings. The greatest difficulty was knowing when to leave without appearing churlish.

When the conversations got beyond the initial politeness stage, I usually asked if I could switch on the tape recorder. People always agreed, and wanted to hear their own voices played back before settling down to talk. I did not prepare interview schedules, but usually explained what I would like us to discuss. Some of these audiotapes last for two hours or more. I did not transcribe them all, but listened several times over, making copious notes, then selected specific extracts to transcribe. I gave copies of the transcripts to the families concerned, and only very rarely had any comments in return. But it was obvious on subsequent visits that people had read them. Sometimes, they wanted to discuss further issues which had been raised.

The interviews with the teachers were somewhat more formally organised. I asked Janet and Sandra if they wanted to be interviewed together but they both preferred to be interviewed singly. This we did in my house during the summer holiday, after I had known them for about 18 months. I prepared a general schedule, which I showed each of them at the start of the interview and then left in sight between us, but did not refer to directly again. Both interviews turned into long and, at times, very personal conversations. Again, I gave them both copies of the notes from their own interviews, and they duly gave me permission to use parts of the material. Both Janet and Sandra were very modest, but I like to think they were happy to have their voices and viewpoints recorded in this way.

Securing interviews with middle school teachers was more complicated, but I finally managed to sit down with four of them, all women, with tea and cake after school one day. The teachers were frank and honest in expressing their views – so frank, in fact, that they gave me two serious methodological problems, one during the interview and one afterwards. Some of the views expressed in the interview were based on factual inaccuracies. Some assertions could even possibly have been construed as racist.

In the course of the interview, I had had to keep very quiet, and mentally do one of Peshkin's (1988) 'subjectivity audits'. Should I have intervened and put the teachers right on the facts on which they were basing their negative views of the children and their families? Afterwards, the question I faced was: what was I to do with these data? Should I expose them and their factual errors which, in a sense, I had a right to do as the interviewees had given me their 'informed consent'?

The first thing I did was take my problem to the intercollegiate research group. A lively and forthright discussion helped me to see that my role as a researcher in this instance was not (to repeat Geertz's words – see Chapter One) to 'strike back and reform' but to 'record'. I wasn't claiming to have found 'the truth', and my responsibility as an ethnographer was to tell the stories I had found.

I gave transcripts of the interview to each of the participants and asked if there were any sections they wanted me to remove, and there weren't. When I eventually wanted to use sections of this interview in my book, I sought advice from several people I trusted and followed it as carefully as I could. But I still worry that I may have caused offence or hurt people's feelings.

8

Honour and authenticity:
the methodology chapter

Chris Kearney

Full accountability, of course, like the dream of self knowledge, is
elusive. James Clifford 1997:11

Although the earlier part of the project went relatively
smoothly for me, the methodology chapter proved to be a
real struggle. Most people I talked to said that they did their
methodology chapter near the end. Eve was insistent that I start
reading and thinking about it from the beginning. As I said in
Chapter Two, my journals reveal that she was recommending books
on methodology to me at my first tutorial with her. In retrospect I
think she was right, but at the time I had little understanding of
what it meant or why it was important. In my MA I had not dealt
with such issues. Yet an understanding of methodological problems
provides the basis of how to construct your argument and describe
the kind of truth you are telling. It is the basis of how you convince
your readers that you are giving a reliable picture of what is going on
in the lives of the people you are studying. Moreover, it helps you to
be explicit about the ways in which you explore the patterns and
deal with the inevitable dilemmas which occur. In short it is the
justification of your approach.

But it does something more than this. It forces us be explicit about the links between important perspectives in our lives: the personal, the professional, the philosophical and the political. It affects the research in a profound way. It permeates the work. If our narratives and arguments are going to be convincing to others then we have to be clear about why the topic is important; how it furthers our own understanding of the issues and how we deal with them in practice. It also clarifies why it is important to those involved in the study; how our relationship can be as collusive and symbiotic as possible and finally why it is important to public policy in terms of justice and equality. Methodology enables us to gain that clarity. But what does 'methodology' mean?

Methodology is not method

Eve had a mantra: 'Methodology is not the same thing as method'. Yet it confused me that it had some method in it. It took me a very long time to grasp that, and there are days even now where I'm not entirely sure about the distinction. I guess that the methods are the tools we use to establish patterns and examine our evidence, whereas methodology is our justification of why we use certain tools in preference to others and why we have decided upon particular combinations of methods and approaches to examine the particular phenomenon in question.

The two books Eve recommended in that first session were by Silverman (1993) and Alasuutari (1995). Of the two, I found Alasuutari more accessible and less abstract. That suited me in the early stages. I appreciated Silverman's books later on. Alasuutari used the helpful term 'unriddling', which described succinctly the complex process of examining culture and identity. He also eschewed notions of purity, and this chimed in well with my own understandings. It also opened up possibilities of using a variety of approaches from theoretical disciplines, which are sometimes viewed as conflicting and mutually exclusive. He calls this approach 'bricolage'. With this way of working you could use statistical surveys to enhance the understanding of more narrative-based methods, which would require less positivistic analysis. More importantly he demonstrated to me how working with a very small sample and analysing their stories in depth could illuminate larger questions of culture and identity:

Even the seemingly most individualistic interpretations of the world are never truly and thoroughly unique. On the other hand, the 'deep structures' of culture only exist as people act and behave in accordance with those structures or make use of them in their activity. Indeed the line of enquiry known as cultural studies is best described as a crossroads, the arrival, through the application of concepts from various disciplines, at a shared view that it is useful to study cultural distinctions and meaning systems from the point of view of both actors and structures. (1995: 35)

My own problem was compounded by the fact that my study was not strictly ethnographic. My own reading is wide-ranging and eclectic and my own view is holistic. So there's a problem. In an early notebook, after my first interview with Aliki, I tried to sort out the different areas covered by our talk. They were broad and I note that they include:

Ethnographic – concepts of culture and identity

Philosophical – ethics (values) and epistemology (concepts of learning and knowledge)

Geopolitics – concepts of power, movement, dispersion, dispossession and the role of the mass media

Narrative – the stories are a text

Psychology – stories point to inner struggles, conflicts and contradictions.

My methodological problems were further exacerbated by the fact that, like all academic disciplines, ethnography is not a monolithic phenomenon. It has its own cultures, factions and cliques which have widely differing values and philosophies and pursue different agendas. I guess that there are few (if any) pure academic disciplines. So who could guide me through the maze?

Van Maanen (1988), already mentioned, makes a spirited defence of the qualitative approaches I was following. This early reading had a profound yet only half conscious influence on me while I was sorting out my conference paper 'Deep Excavations' (later published in the *Journal of Inclusive Education* (1998a). By this time I had conducted my first three interviews and had read a great deal of work in the area of cultural studies. I felt it expressed and analysed the complexity and contradictions, which were appearing in the interviews I was conducting. These contradictions are summarised eloquently by Ien Ang (1994: 18):

> The post-modern ethnicity can no longer be experienced as naturally based upon tradition and ancestry, it must be a provisional and partial site of identity, which must be constantly (re)invented and (re)negotiated...In short, if I am inescapably Chinese by descent I am only sometimes Chinese by consent. When and how is a matter of politics.

The three interviews I had conducted provided me with fascinating narratives. I had to find a way of clarifying what was said, discovering patterns without oversimplifying what I had found out. But to do that, I had to tackle the issue of methodology head on.

The genesis of the methodology chapter

Around this time, Eve let me know about a conference in ethnographic methodologies. It was to be held at the University of Georgia in early 1998 and I drafted a proposal for a paper. This gave me the impetus I needed. I had to explain what I intended to do. I also was forced to make a first stab at the chapter for the thesis. Once I had written the paper it changed very little when I delivered my thesis to Senate House in 2001. Here is the introductory paragraph from my final draft.

> In the current interconnected and mass mediated world, notions of culture, community and identity are complex, multifaceted, often contradictory and difficult to describe. Furthermore, ways in which research is conducted are becoming increasingly problematic. This is particularly true of those ethnographic studies which seek to provide a platform for dispossessed and marginalised groups: those within the community whose voices are sidelined or diminished through powerful institutions such as the media. Although most educational systems speak the rhetoric of equality of opportunity, turning this into a reality in terms of either the recruitment and retention of 'ethnic minority' teachers or the content of the curriculum seems to present persistent problems and dilemmas. At one point it appeared that educational research may present a solution. I am thinking particularly of the rise of anti-racist initiatives and the development of sociolinguistics. Often such works, particularly in

the field of ethnography have attempted to present a collaborative approach. This research project itself follows such a pattern.

In this chapter I shall describe the methodological problems which I faced in attempting to 'unriddle' the interviews with six bilingual/bicultural people. I shall explain why I have preferred some research methods over others and I shall discuss some of the strengths and limitations of those I have chosen. This is because I think we need to be as full and candid as possible about the conduct and context of the research. In my view a warts and all approach to our writing which includes an admission of the messiness of the process can only help to do justice to the complexity of the phenomena we are describing. We are an important part of the research and it is much more useful if we do not cover our tracks. Those tracks are, in my opinion, central to the story.

Then I listed some of my concerns:

Collaboration has a cosy ring about it. But like its travelling companion, partnership, it has some troubling aspects. Both notions raise deeper and more aggravating questions. Questions which probe the aspects of power which tend to lie, unexamined, at the heart of the research.

In conducting ethnographic research some of the major issues are:

■ Who owns the research?

■ What is the role of the university-based researcher?

■ How can the work be conducted ethically?

■ How far can it be truly collaborative given the inbuilt discrepancies in the power relationships?

■ How can we ensure that our joint efforts compose as authentic a picture as possible of such a complex social reality which links history, culture, identity through the mind and memory maps of individual consciousness?

To do this, I had two main problems. Firstly, I had to limit my scope in terms of the areas to be studied. Ethnography was certainly a feature of my approach, but so were other areas such as autobiography and social psychology. It then occurred to me that all could be subsumed under the umbrella of life history/autobiography. This meant that both the methodology and my unriddling would focus upon autobiographical narrative and I should use narrative analysis as my main tool. But first there were broader methodological concerns to consider.

There were several individuals and texts that helped me gain a clearer picture of what I was doing and why. As well as Aalasuutari and Silverman, Eve introduced me to a paper called 'Advancing Phenomenography' by Francis (1993) which had a profound effect upon the way in which I conducted the interviews. Francis considered that the interviewee needed to take the initiative totally and advocated unstructured conversations:

> The aim of the interview is to have the interviewee thematise the phenomenon of interest and make the thinking explicit. (1993:70)

This resonated with my approaches in educational drama and, although I did not slavishly follow her approach, it certainly was a major consideration in the conduct of interviews and proved to elicit very rich and interesting narratives.

General methodological distinctions

About the same time, Eve gave me a chapter entitled 'Ethnographic Methodologies' by Kamil, Langer and Shanahan (1985:72) which provided a useful table that distinguishes between experimental and ethnographic research methods.

Major distinctions between ethnographic and experimental enquiry

Ethnographic inquiry	Experimental enquiry
A. Phenomenological base Seeks to understand human behaviour from participant's frame of reference	**A.** Positivist base Seeks to learn facts and identify causes
B. Systematically observes recurring patterns of behaviour as people engage in regularly occurring activities	**B.** Sets variables that need to be understood in relation to each other – some (independent) can be manipulated to determine their effects on others (dependent)
C. Identifies and describes phenomena from beginning to end across cycles	**C.** Tests relationships

D. Develops hypotheses grounded in the event and driven by the conceptual framework of the study	**D**. Preformulates research questions or hypotheses
E. Uses field setting that can be further tested with naturalistic experiments	**E**. Uses laboratory or field settings
F. Confirms findings across a variety of information sources, contexts and time	**F**. Computes interrater and statistical probability

This clarified for me why I preferred certain approaches. Up until this point my preferences were more intuitive than explicit. Each of these viewpoints emanates from a different philosophical tradition. Experimental approaches tend to stem from the positivist view (Comte, 1973; Durkheim, 1956), which seeks to identify facts and causes. Scientific approaches have their roots in 18th century European speculations from such thinkers as Newton, Locke and Descartes. Such notions continue to have a powerful position in defining what is hard, scientific and valid in academic research in academic circles. They continue to be seen by many as the only systematic scientific approach. Although the table above provides a broad set of distinctions which are useful, the link between ethnography and phenomenology is by no means simple and straightforward.

At one of the Saturday schools for post graduate students held by Goldsmiths, Diana Coben, who was Head of the Postgraduate Programme, gave a presentation where she clarified a further misconception I held. Up to that point I had considered positivism as virtually synonymous with empiricism. She pointed out that, because it was dealing with observable phenomena, ethnographic research was also empirical. This was a real breakthrough for me and it made Alaasutari's approach of 'bricolage' all the more useful.

Methodological dilemmas in ethnography

There are always some texts which are more important than others and it was around this time that I discovered Clifford's book, *The Predicament of Culture* (1988). Not only did I find it a totally absorbing work, written in a lively accessible style; it revolutionised my view of ethnography and provided the basis for the ethnographic part of the methodology chapter. He set the whole issue of ethnographic research in an historical context and provided a critical overview of some of the main theorists. In the paper I wrote for the conference I stated that:

> Clifford's work provides an interesting critical framework by which we may be able to mitigate the worst excesses of the colonial legacy in the ethnographic method. This is because he:

> ■ locates ethnography in its historical context

> ■ provides an overview of the strengths and limitations of its main theorists

> ■ situates ethnography inextricably within colonial forms of discourse

> ■ is transparent about ethnographers and their baggage of assumed values and beliefs

> ■ links his thinking to notions of polyphonic discourses, which were developed by Bakhtin

> ■ links it to major movements in Western Art and literature, particularly surrealism, to provide some understanding of cross cultural creation

> ■ is specific about the influence of power on conceptions of self and identity

> ■ sees deliberate constructions of identity as ways individuals balance and accommodate such competing discourses

> ■ encourages us to see travel as important an ingredient of culture as settlement.

> If we temper our ethnographic methods with these notes of both insight and caution, they may still prove to be useful tools. He concludes:

> In the last decades of the twentieth century, ethnography begins from the inescapable fact that Westerners are not the only ones going places in the modern world....But have not travellers always encountered worldly 'natives'? Strange anticipation: the English Pilgrims arrive at Plymouth Rock in the New world only to find Squanto, a Patuxet, just back from Europe. (Clifford, 1988: 17)

For me this was reassurance that I was on the right lines. It helped me to discover appropriate analytical tools. Most significantly he had demolished the notion of the pure informant as a persistent myth. The other book which was a major influence on my thinking here was Clifford Geertz's (1988) *Works and Lives*, which examines the writings of major anthropologists as literary texts. In it, Geertz demolishes the myth of anthropology as some kind of objective science and reveals that representation is a problem of writing. The historical and sociocultural approach of both books provided a key as to how I should approach the methodological problems surrounding life histories and autobiography.

The problem of analysing autobiographical narratives

For this section of the methodology chapter, I drew on a collection of articles edited by Hatch and Wisenieska (1995) entitled *Life History and Narrative*. Their individual papers pose interesting questions and ethical dilemmas for researchers in the field. Here is how I made sense of them in my final version:

> As with ethnography there are problems and dilemmas involved in making sense of the stories themselves. To begin with it is worth examining the obvious advantages to this approach.
>
>> Life history and narrative offer exciting alternatives for connecting lives and stories of individuals to the understanding of larger human and social phenomena (Hatch and Wisniewski, 1995)
>>
>> A life history is composed of self-referential stories through which the author-narrator constructs the identity and point(s) of view of a unique individual historically situated in culture, time and place
>
> It is also a critical approach. As Goodson (1995, in Hatch and Wisenieska) states
>
>> These approaches offer a serious opportunity to question the implicit racial, class or gender biases which existing modes of enquiry mystify whilst reproducing (See Giroux, 1991).
>>
>> Storying and narratology are genres that move researchers beyond (or to the side of) the main paradigms of inquiry with their numbers, variables, psychometrics, psychologisms, and decontextualised theories

But he warns us to be vigilant of 'the tyranny of the local' (Harvey, 1989) and cites Denzin's timely advice that:

> The cultural logics of late capitalism valorise the life story, autobiographical document because they keep the myth of the autonomous individual alive. The logic of the confession reifies the concept of self and turns it into a cultural commodity... The recent return of the life story celebrates the importance of the individual under the conservative politics of late postmodernism. (1992: 8-9)

This is one of the major problems of postmodernist theorising. The lack of a grand narrative or even a clearly delineated set of common political and social aims or values can put you in the camp of the people who have come to dispossess you.

As with the problem of informants in ethnographic research we must be cautious about generalisation we can make from these sources. In their paper, 'Life history and narrative: Questions, issues and exemplary works', Hatch and Wiseniewski (1995) asked narrative and life history scholars to comment on their own work. The analysis of their responses resulted in them raising a number of interesting issues and perspectives ie:

- life histories as a type of narrative

- stories as ways of knowing

- life histories as individual, contextually situated stories

- how life histories are distinguished from other types of qualitative research by:

  - their focus on the individual

  - the personal nature of the research process

  - the emphasis on subjectivity.

It is also worth noting that, in common with ethnography, life history is also a genre developed through a Western/European literary tradition. It is not natural and unselfconscious, despite its personal form. In the earliest writings, lives of public figures were formal and exterior, revealing little of the individual's private and personal thoughts. As Bakhtin (1981) notes, the Ancient Greeks did not use the form extensively. It was only during the later Graeco-Roman period that autobiography developed. Even then Ovid, Horace and

Juvenal tended to treat the form ironically. Confessional literature only really began with St Augustine, so that the model we have internalised stems directly from this source. Much of the commentary on this aspect has been from the field literary criticism. It is closely related to the autobiographical novel, or 'spiritual autobiography' of such writers as Defoe.

As part of my MA I had studied the traditions of autobiography in the Western canon. Part of the problem of autobiography is its apparent naturalness. Spengmann (1980) was particularly helpful, setting it in a wider context and showing how its historical developments were cumulative and have added to the richness of the genre. Equally they reflect the preoccupations current at the time and place of their invention. He makes the interesting point that Augustine's work posed problems in the conduct of autobiographical writing. They are ones which are only too familiar to me as I try to unriddle the interviews. They are:

How can the self know itself? Can it be achieved:

■ by surveying in the memory its completed past actions from an unmoving point above them?

■ by moving inquisitively through its own memories and ideas to some conclusion about them?

■ by performing a sequence of symbolic actions, through which the ineffable self can be realised?

Such problems are closely linked to the identified categories: historical, philosophical and poetic.

Making sense of stories

The second major breakthrough in this area was discovering that this cultural form of narrative is the major way in which we make sense of the inchoate simultaneous experience of day-to-day living. Suzanne Langer (1941: 262) points out that this is the way we shape reality; by narrating our memories. This in turn led me to the central methodological problems of validity and reliability.

Two books, which coincidently bore the title *Narrative Analysis* helped me most. The one by Cortazzi (1993) critically analysed various approaches in a comprehensive and systematic manner.

The other, by Reissman (1983:64) was a concentrated and critical overview of how feminist researches had analysed narratives, mainly life histories. Reissman articulates this position well when she states:

> The historical truth of an individual's account is not the primary issue. Narrativisation *assumes* point of view... Narratives are laced with social discourses and power relations over time... *Trustworthiness not 'truth'* is the key semantic difference. The latter assumes an objective reality, whereas the former moves the process into the social world. (my emphases)

Most significantly for me, she gave the most convincing set of criteria in checking the validity and reliability of her accounts. She suggests that in our research we seek illumination of this complex phenomenon and do not limit our investigation to the construction of narrow paradigms, which exclude point of view. She goes on to suggest four criteria for approaching validity in narrative inquiry:

persuasiveness: is it reasonable and convincing?

correspondence: can it be taken back to the researched?

coherence: does it provide a coherent picture of the situation described?

pragmatic: to what extent can we act upon it?

Through this I realised that I would have to devise frameworks which would help me capture the complexity and contradiction apparent in the narratives. Moreover I realised that it was a problem of representation and that meant a problem of writing.

How reliable is it?

This, in turn, related to the deeper problem of reliability. As it was, I was examining that most unreliable of phenomena – memory. How could that be rendered persuasive? Here I returned to the notion of 'trustworthiness not truth'. Through Cortazzi I encountered the useful idea of 'repisodic memory', a phrase coined by Neisser (Fivush and Neisser, 1996) when he was analysing the reliability and validity of the testimony of John Dean at the Watergate hearings. John Dean was dubbed the 'human tape recorder' because of his allegedly phenomenal memory. Neisser found this was not the case but developed the idea that, although memory may not be precise in its grasp of detail, it may still be honest and trustworthy. He contends that, if we have a series of conversations with someone on the same topic over a period of time, we may not be able to remember what was related at specific times. However, we will remember the salient features and general themes when we relate them to others. Trustworthiness not truth is the key.

From then on, I realised that my main problems were not of notions of objective truth but how faithfully and ethically to represent and analyse the information I had been given. As I say in my title, it was a matter of honour and authenticity. I owed a debt of honour to the individuals who had spoken to me of intimate aspects of their lives to stay as close to their intended meanings as possible. That is to present as authentic as possible a picture of the changes they were experiencing at that stage of their lives within my own constraints and limitations as a writer. The process of establishing a convincing picture of what was going on was a complex one. I realised it was about representation too. In this case it was a problem of writing. I had done the thinking, now I had to test it out in public. In Georgia.

Coda: Georgia winter light

The weather in Georgia was cold and keen. Icy winds stirred the confederate flags displayed above the porches of some of the timber-framed houses in Athens. The shuttle from the airport had detoured through several outlying villages, which seemed to exhibit in rapid succession union flags and confederate flags. Were they still fighting the civil war? The university of Georgia covers a substantially larger space than the town of Athens, where it is situated. The town consists of low-rise houses and shops laid out in a grid system. The campus consists of large red-brick faculty buildings set out in a rolling green landscape of well-manicured lawns. The methodology conference was held in a building specifically designed for external work and contained accommodation for delegates. It is the only time I have actually stayed in a conference venue.

Due to snowstorms to the north of Georgia, many of the more local delegates could not attend. All the same, there were plenty of interesting people and I presented my paper. It was very well received. Presenting a paper can provide an enormous boost to your confidence and you get to meet others who are working in similar areas and grappling with similar problems. Attending their sessions and asking questions can often give you ideas and new approaches to your own work. You also get some constructive criticism and suggestions. They really help to sharpen and focus the work. This happened to me.

Jim Scheurich was using video to chart radical democratic approaches to the education of migrant workers in Texas. The videos were produced in close collaboration with the workers and their families. I also met Christina, a Latina from Canada, who was using her autobiography to explore the complexity of her identity. Her thesis included personal photographs. She had presented her thesis as a piece of performance art.

So many possibilities opened up for me. It was here that I first encountered the work of Denzin, Lincoln, Guba and Tierney. I bought several of their books. I came home. I refined my paper in the light of what I had learned in cold, cold Georgia. It became the methodology chapter and remained pretty much unchanged when I presented my thesis three years later. My mind was clear. The way was now open for me to analyse the work in depth.

9

Negotiating methodologies

Aura Mor-Sommerfeld

People have always wanted (and needed) to understand, and sometimes to generalise, about aspects of human behaviour(s) in order to explain certain phenomena. Experience, intuition and common sense have all been used and exercised to this end. These old generalisations are to be found in aphorisms such as 'a trouble shared is a trouble halved', or 'we'll cross that bridge when we come to it', known and used in different cultures. On the one hand, it seems that people are helped by such explanations but, on the other, we might ask: does it really help people to share their troubles, and is it right to think about crossing a bridge only when we come to it? It seems that daily experience and intuition might lead us to contradictory generalisations and opposing conclusions, without being able to decide between them and, if we do not look carefully, without being able to understand them ...

That was the introduction to the methodology chapter of my thesis. I continued:

Professional researchers have traditionally tried to formulate human behaviour patterns in order to explain and to predict them. Using various methods, researchers try to overcome problems endemic to inquiries that are based on experience, intuition and commonsense. Under the heading of 'research methods' we can find a number of activities, beginning with formulating a question or assumption which refers to a specific social phenomenon; examining all relevant data in order to explain that phenomenon, find answers to questions, and/or support the assumptions. But is generalisation the ultimate goal? Can we only explain phenomena, understand procedures or help to build new insights by generalising?

According to Kerlinger (1972), the explanation of a phenomenon becomes a theory. Kerlinger suggests that:

> ... a theory is a set of interrelated constructs (concepts), definitions, and propositions that presents a systematic view of phenomena by specifying relations among variables, with the purpose of explaining and predicting these phenomena. (Kerlinger, 1972 :11)

But is that all? What else induces us to establish a theory? What helps us to recognise and to evaluate it?

Ely *et al.* (1997) state that:

> ... one's research stance, one's framework for thinking and doing in light of the spirit of a theoretical position, must be a conscious choice... to amalgamate it with others, to create one's own, to select another and begin all over again. Thus, symbolic interaction, critical ethnography, phenomenology, action research, hermeneutics, and case study, among others, become alternatives and possibilities rather than rigid corsets. (1997: 33)

For them, 'this is a liberating view' (Ely *et al*, 1997: 33). This 'liberating view' becomes crucial and central when writing a thesis. Qualitative research enables the researcher to free the language, especially in terms of writing, and it seems that the ethnographic approach also includes such a belief and such a value. The language selected (words, structure) assists us to approach this view, and thus it becomes not just a means but also a goal in itself. Any approach, any methodology involves political perspectives, philosophical attitudes, social approaches and cultural norms. All of these aspects were and still are involved in the methods I selected for my study.

The beginning was not at all simple. Although I had decided on a qualitative research, I had little idea about the methodology I would be using, having no expertise in this area. But my supervisor did have that experience, and she inspired me with her confidence; she directed me to the field of ethnography, and step by step I began to construct my understanding and I can even say my identity as a researcher. Almost from the beginning I could understand that the methodology must be considered when *thinking* about a research; that it is essential and central to the design of the study, and connected to data analysis; that it is one of its germs, and that it is integral to the whole context of the research. I understood then that through the methodology, a researcher vindicates their argument, and that if the methodology is faulty, the whole research will also fail. All this required careful thought, much work, some daring, and a willingness to achieve results through trial and error. I think I still needed some time to fully comprehend this notion.

All of this influenced my reading. I read about methodology, research, models of studies, and data analysis. Among many others, I reviewed Apple (1989), Flick (1998), Gregory (1990, 1996), Hammersley and Atkinson (1997), Heath (1982 a) and b), Hymes (1996), Jordan and Yeomans (1995), Ochs (1979), Silverman (1993). Some of these authors (e.g. Gregory, Heath) focus on their own studies; some of them (such as Flick or Silverman) write about research in general, while others (Ochs, for example) concentrate on a particular methodology. Reading about researches and methodologies helped me to formulate and design my own.

But reading and talking – it helps to talk about one's research as much as possible – about *ethnography* was not enough. Something was missing. Then, during one of our meetings my supervisor suggested that I consider *ethnomethodology*, and combine it with ethnography in my study. This was how I discovered Garfinkel's *Studies in Ethnomethodology* (1967). At about the same time, in an interesting journal called *TEXT*, I found the final link: a brilliant article by McDermont and Tylbour (1983) called 'On the Necessity of Collusion', discussing a collusive research. This was the turning point. Thus the combination between ethnography and ethnomethodology, and the small but very significant addition of the *collusive approach*, became the means by which I negotiated my methodology.

I am trying to present here what I did, from the beginning of designing the study up to writing the chapter on methodology, by combining the issues of what, why and how:

■ what methods I used and what they meant for my work

■ why I chose these methods

■ how I used and wrote the final methodology chapter in my work.

Actually writing that chapter was what finally helped me to establish my theory about new language acquisition. My two previous chapters (three and six) set out the context – both personal and professional – of my study. Now I describe the study itself, after which I return to some theoretical aspects regarding the methodologies, and some examples of how I used them.

Designing the study: connecting to the context

Ethnographic research usually focuses on one group. It was Heath who (in 1982c) first provided us with a comparative study based on ethnographic methods. In 'What No Bedtime Story Means: Narrative Skills at Home and School', Heath describes two very different communities: Trackton and Roadville, in the Appalachian Mountain region of the United States. When summarising her work, Heath writes, relying on Hymes (1973) that:

> ... we need, in short, a great deal of ethnography to provide descriptions of the way different social groups 'take' knowledge from the environment .... Literacy events must also be interpreted in relation to the *larger sociocultural patterns* which they may exemplify or reflect. (1982c:182)

I studied two groups; not just because of Heath's and Hymes' conclusions, but because of the complexity of the political and sociocultural situation in Israel. In my opinion, discussing the data concerning two different communities amplifies Heath's argument and presents a dialectical, analytical approach to this study.

As I have already explained, I was searching for answers to the questions of how young children develop literacy in a second-new language in the formal context of school, and how best to help them to develop that language. My research took place in two schools in two discrete communities, one of L1 Hebrew speakers and the other of L1 Arabic speakers. My purpose was not to judge the two communities but to examine and compare them in order to gain a better understanding of the topic by looking at both of them.

In the course of three years, up to four times a month, sometimes even on consecutive days, I met children from the two schools mentioned above. I observed, talked with and listened to young children and their teachers who were using children's books to learn or teach English as a new language. During that time I recorded and documented the children's discussions between themselves and with their teachers about languages, books, stories and literacy. I collected written material from both the children and their teacher, about the children and about language lessons, and I followed their progress in reading, writing, and developing a new language. At some of the meetings, it was the teacher who conducted the lesson. On other occasions, I took over, in my role as participating observer.

When I first met the children they were about six years old, in first grade. I accompanied them through their school years up to the third grade. During the first eighteen months I visited the schools less often – only once or twice a month – than I did during the second half of the second year and the third year (when it was three to four times a month). Although I focused only on a small group in each class, in both cases the rest of the class was interested, involved in, and influenced by the group's activities. In both schools I acquired some of my data from the whole class, especially at the beginning of my investigation. As my study continued, I became interested also in the teachers' instruction. When I began my study I defined this as part of the research, but as my work progressed, it became a subject in its own right. Indeed, learning cannot take place without learners, though it frequently occurs without teachers. But when a good teacher is involved in the process, the likelihood of success increases significantly. This insight both influenced and was influenced by my methodology.

The following principles formed the basis of my study, and guided me when *collecting data*. All have arisen from the theories mentioned earlier and are concisely reviewed in the following sections.

Guiding principles
■ *using authentic texts*: children's literature
■ *enabling*: options for *personal-selection*: books, topics, tasks
■ *sharing*: ideas, attitudes

- *observing*: (and being participant observer): *what* is going on, and *how*? *thinking: why*?
- *listening*: who says what, why; what is the *meaning*?
- *dialogue and negotiation*: between children, between teachers (adults) and children, between researcher (me) and children and/or teachers
- *considering (ways of working with)*: individuals, pairs, groups (small, large)
- *reflection*: (through) documentation, discussion.

These principles are integral to what I called the 'C' connection of my study: *Context, Conflict, Concept, Community, Communication, Culture* and *Common-sense* and they were discussed in the context of data analysis in separate and specific chapters in my thesis. They are all represented in the negotiated methodologies and fit well with my values.

Ethnography: learning, knowing and understanding a culture

Ethnography ... is carried out, above all, with love, and furthermore, with an intimate awareness of the nuances of local idiom, and with sense of the overall unity of the culture, and with a desire to preserve it. (Gellner, 1998:132)

This sensitive definition of ethnography does not simplify matters. On the contrary, it creates a greater obligation, a need to assess the advantages and limitations very carefully.

The title of this section 'Learning and Understanding a Culture' could just as well be 'The Culture of Learning to Know and Understand'. After all, learning, knowing, and understanding are a type of culture; so is doing research.

Let us look at other ethnographers' views:

Ethnography is the study of people's behaviour in naturally occurring, ongoing settings, with a focus on cultural interpretation of behaviour. (Watson-Gegeo, 1988: 575)

[Ethnography's] goal is to describe the ways of living of a social group... By becoming a participant in the social group, an ethnographer attempts to record and describe the overt, manifest, and explicit behaviours and values and tangible items of culture...

Ethnographers attempt to learn the language of the society, and the structures and functions of cultural components, before attempting to recognise patterns of behaviour that may be covert, ideal, and implicit to members of the culture. Ethnographers attempt to learn the conceptual framework of members of the society and to organise materials on the basis of boundaries understood by those being observed. (Heath, 1982a:34)

Based on Heath, Watson-Gegeo (1988) sees the ethnographer's goal as:

... to provide a description and an interpretive-explanatory account of what people do in a setting (such as a classroom, neighbour-hood, or community), the outcome of their interactions, and the way they understand what they are doing. (Watson-Gegeo, 1988: 576)

Learning, knowing and understanding are thus crucial terms in ethnography, along with behaviour, observation recognition, setting and patterns. They all fit the concept of seeing understanding as a phenomenon of shared meaning, which is also accepted by sociolinguists (Becker, 1986).

In my work, the terms 'knowledge', 'behaviour', 'understanding' and 'shared meaning' were applied to young children developing a new language through literacy. The questions I asked then might express this appropriately: 1) How do we find out and explain what children *know* about other languages? 2) How do they *behave* in and through the process of *learning*, and what is the meaning of their *behaviour*? 3) How does *understanding* become a phenomenon of *shared meaning*? I have discovered that these aspects of knowledge and understanding involve the researcher and the subjects of the research in a common aim.

In this book, my co-writers discuss ethnography, its importance, the way they dealt with it and the additional methodology they used in order to accomplish their study. I find the fact that all of us needed another methodology in addition to ethnography very interesting and significant. In my case, the answer lies in the need to deepen the investigation of the terms 'knowledge', 'making sense' and 'understanding' for which other methodologies could possibly supply more answers.

Here I would like to focus on two of the other methodologies that helped me to establish my theory: ethnomethodology and the collusive approach[1].

Ethnomethodology: phenomenology – society and the individual

Ethnomethodology describes how people make sense in and through the ways they communicate. It focuses on the common sense of everyday life, and the practices (methods) by which we make our actions understandable and able to be shared by others. The term ethnomethodology was coined in 1967 by Garfinkel in order to define social science researchers' shift of attention to examination of practices and procedures. These procedures do not occur as discrete events, but are connected as factors relating to the acts of others, responding and reacting to them, and sometimes anticipating them:

> I use the term 'ethnomethodology' to refer to the investigation of the rational properties of indexical expressions and other practical actions as contingent ongoing accomplishments of organised artful practices of everyday life. (Garfinkel, 1967:11)

Ethnomethodology: views and procedures

As Garfinkel himself states (1967:36n), the philosophy ethnomethodology derives from Schutz's (1962) translation of phenomenology from epistemological to sociological issues. This theory stresses the internal connection between thought and the object of thought, and suggests that our experiences are necessarily connected to the object we are experiencing. Objects do not just exist for themselves. The experience of an object – is modified by circumstances and by the attitude of the person who experiences it.

According to Schutz (1962), meaning is subjective and unique to the individual; and the individuals' subjectivity allows actors participating in a social event to categorise the acts of other actors in order to give them a meaning. Therefore, knowledge about what is going on in social conditions, and hence in the whole world, is involved with constructions of interpretations which are eventually interpreted as facts. Thus, ethnomethodology refers to what people do to confirm that something exists. It assumes that everyone has her/his own patterns for constructing meaning (meaning depends on doing, not on abstract ideas), that these patterns result from the contexts in which they occur, and there are no preconceived ideas or predictions of results: like actors on a stage – removed from reality though eventually, in most cases, it becomes the reality itself. (Garfinkel, 1967; Heritage, 1984; Hilbert, 1993; Coulon, 1995). According to Schutz (1962) reality, as we see it, is the world of common sense, the socio-cultural world. But it is no more real than other aspects of meaning which we might have chosen.

Garfinkel claimed that it is impossible to ignore operational structures. He argued that the way to understand reality is:

> ... by seeking to establish the presence, in the conversationalists' relationship, of warranting virtues such as their having spoken honestly, openly, candidly, sincerely and the like. All of which ... would invoke... what the parties understood in common. (Garfinkel, 1967:27)

Ethnographic literature describes the learning environment and the interaction between individuals within that environment; but it obviously cannot examine individual thoughts and doings as they occur in that environment. Ethnomethodology thus refers to the specific behaviour, both oral and non-oral, with which the participants respond to the social order which they create together (Varenne and McDermott, 1998). From Garfinkel's point of view, learning and culture are imposed on reality; they are 'attempts to come to terms with practical circumstances as a texture of relevances over the continuing occasions of interpersonal transactions' (Garfinkel, 1967:175).

The influence of this approach on ethnographic research is its emphasis on analysis of the immense input invested in creating one small extract from day-by-day circumstances. McDermott and Roth (1978) stress that:

> ... it is axiomatic within anthropology that a culture or social structure forms a context for the individual who has to operate in the context... there is no escape from the careful and detailed analysis of how people together organise their behaviour from one moment to another. (1978:338)

They suggest seeing organisations as day-by-day achievements, and day-by-day initiatives of logical ways to attain those achievements. The methods by which all of these procedures are seen and examined, and which is so often mentioned in the same breath with ethnomethodology is conversation analysis.

Conversation analysis

Conversation analysis is a method of studying the sequential structure and coherence of everyday conversation by employing techniques of ethnomethodology. Conversation analysis (CA) 'emerged out of Garfinkel's (1967) programme for ethnomethodology and its analysis of 'folk' ('ethno') methods' (Silverman, 1993: 120). Like them, Coulon suggests that, since conversation analysis is far from the usual sociological inquiry, it has sometimes been 'considered to be an autonomous field, separated from ethnomethodology' (Coulon, 1995:38).

The CA approach studies recordings of real conversations to establish what properties are used in a systematic way when people interact linguistically, and is basically empirical, inductive study, grounded in an attempt to describe people's methods for producing orderly social interaction. According to Heritage (1984) the three fundamental assumptions of conversation analysis are:

1. interaction is structurally organised

2. the contributions of participants to this interaction are contextually oriented: the indexing process of utterances to a context is inevitable

3. these two properties are actualised in every detail of the interaction, so that no detail can be disposed of as being accidental or inaccurate. (Heritage, 1984: 241)

A

Teacher:	Today, we are going to read this book.
Child A:	This is in English
Teacher:	How do you *know*?
Child A:	I know, everyone knows.
Teacher:	Do you want to read this book?

.....

B

Child B: They ask something and then they answer.
Teacher: How do you *know*?

A and B are taken from a formal context of a classroom environment (1, 2, 3). The participants are the teacher, her pupils (L1 Hebrew speakers, 6-7 years old) and the book as the third actor (1, 2, 3). The structure of the conversation is organised – a) by the question-answer pattern; b) by the specific question ('how do you know?') which the teacher asks (1 – structurally organised; 2 – contribution of participants which is contextually oriented). This reveals how the structure's organisation (1) within the context (2) is actualised in every detail of the interaction (3).

The collusive approach

I have identified the discovery of McDermott and Tylbor's (1983) collusive approach as one of the turning points in my work. It enabled me to deepen my understanding of language as a social phenomenon. The collusive approach (from the Latin *colludere*, meaning to play together) describes the connection between ethnomethodology and socio-linguistics, based on the premise that social reality is an ongoing achievement – the result of hard work, routine activity and a covert understanding between social participants. As Garfinkel (1967) points out, it is impossible to understand speech except within social interaction. Owing to the connection between speech and social context, the social meaning becomes reflexive, i.e. no expression is ever complete or clear.

Language provides us with a wide range of labels for any object or act. The social meaning of such terms changes according to circumstances. The ability to understand them is based on common or shared knowledge. Ethnomethodology analyses the construction of this knowledge. The collusive approach to considering language describes how members of social organisations constantly help each other to understand their social circumstances. According to McDermott and Tylbour, this understanding develops within an intricate and ramified concept of a context. It rejects the traditional approach, which sees meaning/intention as the only goal, and recognises the fact that the route towards meaning through speech is never simple, certain, nor clear. It addresses the essence of behaviour and of expression, and the possible connections between them. Evaluation of richness of language and those who hold the language is as important as evaluation of the subjects that occupy people.

The latest developments in social research point out the existence of communicative patterns in education. They indicate that, although the individual is the focus of learning, learning is not limited only to the individual or to her/his privacy. Learning occurs through transference, adaptation and reflection between the individual and her/his environment, ie within a context. Culture and learning, then, are complementary and united. Learning occurs within a cultural context, and learning and culture develop both through and within the learning process. Collusion, then, is a desire for a basic understanding of context, and it has perfectly fitted both my needs and values.

Thinking through writing: behind the turning point

As a rule, I seldom have crises when writing. The crisis I remember best was when I was writing the methodology chapter of my PhD. Perhaps this is why I feel that this was what taught me the most. What is it about the methodology of ethnography that can make one so excited? Is it because this is when you really discover the power of your research? Or because, as in my case, you feel and understand that you can win this struggle? It certainly was a struggle.

When working on a research project, you come to a point that is, for you, a turning point. For me, negotiating and especially writing methodology was such a point. Apart from the investigation itself, understanding the methodology of my research and being able to use it was both significant and exciting. Perhaps this is what ethnography does: it both teaches and touches you in different and unexpected ways. So when I look back and try to understand why I struggled, I think that it had to do with responsibility. My supervisor used to say that if methodology fails then the whole work fails. I think that if methodology stands firm, and if it succeeds, the benefit is the establishment of a theory.

Ultimately, I wrote two different chapters for the methodology and the design of my research. One chapter reviewed the relevant literature and theoretically established the methodology; the other presented the research environment – the schools and the language used in them, the teachers and the children who participated in my research, and the study and its principles. In two other different chapters I presented the data, analysing them ethnographically and ethnomethodologically. This enabled me to examine (here I quote Hammersley and Atkinson, 1997:238) 'the relationship between concepts and indicators in ethnographic research, and the testing of theoretical ideas by means of the comparative method'.

I have suggested the need for an additional methodology, since ethnography alone did not enable full analysis of my data. In my study I formulated and justified my choice thus:

> If ethnography can be identified with observation, then ethno-methodology can be identified with listening. While ethnography uses an extended approach and longitudinal methods, ethno-methodology can consist of a single lesson...The aim of both is comprehension, and they are probably complementary...

> Ethnomethodology investigates what people say, and what people know (and what they think they know). An extension of this might be not just what *they* know or understand, but what the researcher gathers from her/his collected data...

I believe that the way methodologies negotiate is quite similar to how this chapter and indeed this whole book has been composed: by moving between the doing (ethnomethodology) and the writing (ethnography). They are interwoven in this book.

This chapter begins with quotations from my introduction to the methodology chapter in my dissertation. This is how I ended that introduction:

> In order to establish a theory regarding developing literacy in a new language, this chapter discusses the broad issue of methodology and examines the two qualitative methods – ethnography and ethnomethodology – used in this study. It offers: a) a brief review of some general aspects regarding research in applied linguistics; b) examination of ethnographic methods, focusing on their advantages while considering the disadvantages; c) discussion of ethno-

methodology, its origin and necessity in this research; d) procedures of textual critique and analysis; e) meanings and context in psycholinguistic aspects, representing interactional approaches in social science. An example of how all these aspects find expression is given in a separate section. These issues provide the basis for the continuation of the work.

And so they did.

Note

1   In order to accomplish my theory regarding developing literacy in a new language, I also reviewed and discussed procedures of textual critique and analysis and the meanings and context in their psycholinguistic aspects, representing interactional approaches in social science.

Part four
In conclusion:
policy, professional and
personal development

Introduction:
the pattern that connects
Eve Gregory

> The pattern that connects... a dance of interacting parts only secondarily pegged down by various sorts of physical limits and by those limits which organisms characteristically impose. (Bateson, 1979: 13)

Finding the pattern that connects may sometimes seem like chasing a rainbow. It can be an excruciating business stretching over years. Just when you feel it will never emerge, you suddenly find it. The rest of the writing, although still many months of work, comes quickly and easily. In Jean's words, 'the remaining analysis and putting the whole thesis together seemed to happen fairly quickly' (p139) and for Chris 'the writing came very easy. The voices were fresh in my head... I was on a roll.' (p163)

Yet how to find this pattern? Are there any short cuts? The answer must be 'No' and for a simple reason. If your study aims to understand and present the voices of your participants, they must first echo in your head, and for this to happen demands many hours of listening to or watching tapes, transcribing interviews, examining texts and field-notes. The listening is not passive but a painfully active process, often requiring repeated questioning of your participants to discover what they really mean. All this effort rewards you with a sudden acceleration of your writing and, although much longer, your analysis and concluding chapters can often be completed faster than the pilot study.

However, the conclusion needs careful thought. As Aura observes: 'A conclusion is a serious matter' where 'I may or might' becomes 'I argue' or 'I state'. Although unfair, it is clear that some examiners turn first to your conclusions before embarking on the rest of the study. It is, therefore, crucial to present the meaning and importance of your work for both theory and practice (research, policy and field). To neglect either of these can make your work, however thorough, appear lacking. Yet this homeward stretch is probably the most rewarding part of the work. It is where you finally feel that you own the study, an ownership you should extend to others through the presentation and publication of your work. Jean, Chris and Aura explain how they did this in these final chapters.

10

Unlocking doors:
the importance of the PhD

Jean Conteh

Rounding it off

When I began to understand how ethnography and critical discourse analysis could be linked theoretically and methodologically, it felt as if I had entered the final stage of the project. Indeed, from this point, doing the remaining analysis and putting the whole thesis together seemed to happen fairly quickly. There was a lot of cutting and pasting, but very little new writing to do. I went back through my notebooks and transcripts and selected significant episodes from the interviews and conversations with parents and teachers and from the classroom observations. These were ones which had revealed to me different viewpoints on situations with which I thought I was familiar, particularly in classrooms, or which provided information from home contexts which added dimensions to or explained events in school. I used these examples to support my arguments about the ways success in mainstream classrooms could be seen as differently available to individual children. The actual amount of data which finally appeared in the thesis was very small, given how much I had collected over four years, adding up to 200 hours or so of observation notes (in twelve notebooks) and 70 hours of audiotape. From all of this, I included six extracts in the thesis, representing about two hours' worth of data altogether, and presented some further sections in appendices. Here is a list of the extracts in the order in which they were presented:

- Parts of one 30-minute three-way conversation in the first school classroom

- Extracts from one interview with a parent

- Extracts from two interviews with teachers

- Three short extracts from informal conversations with a group of Year 4 children

- Extracts of a teacher-pupil conversation during one science activity in Year 4

- Extracts of one science lesson in Year 6.

At the time each had occurred in the course of my research, it had struck me as significant in some way, so when I went back and scanned through my whole corpus of data, the extracts virtually selected themselves. Similarly, their analyses had all been developing recursively and cumulatively from my reading and discussions with the teachers and parents, and from presenting work in progress to fellow researchers at the intercollegiate seminar and elsewhere. The six examples and their analyses formed the backbone of the thesis. They were presented in different chapters, interspersed with theoretical and contextual sections. The organisation of all this material did not finally fall into place until the very late stages of the whole project. When it did, it represented an attempt to show within the linear constraints of written text the layeredness and intertextuality of the discourses I had been studying.

When I look back at it now, it seems as if the final stages of the so-called writing-up year progressed rapidly, with very few hitches or setbacks. It was all very cumulative and iterative. Chris has made the point about how little redundancy there was in the material he collected in his notebooks, and I found the same with all the different pieces of writing I had worked on in the course of developing the thesis. Though these all seemed to be quite diffuse, when I laid them out in relation to the data, I could see the pattern of how the pieces fitted together to develop a rounded set of arguments. Finally, the thesis was emerging from all the separate strands of the work and I had a final draft to show Eve.

I had a fairly long wait for my viva and, when it came, it all seemed to happen in a gentle, low key and even muted way, despite my great nervousness. Beforehand, several people had told me that I would be asked to explain what I thought my thesis contributed to the growth of original knowledge. I gave this question much thought, but I could not work out how to answer it in the succinct, cut-and-dried way it seemed to demand. In the thesis, I had developed a model of knowledge as politically and socially situated, co-constructed and open to negotiation. The question about original knowledge seemed to imply a product model, along the lines of what Pring (1976) describes as 'philosophical knowledge', something I had argued against. It made me feel as if I was being asked to add my stone, chipped out of the monolithic rock, to the cairn which represented the ever-growing heap of canonical know-ledge in someone's grand design of things.

But when the viva came round, I was not asked the question, which was a great relief as I still did not know how to answer it. I now know what I would have said if the question had arisen. If my research does make any contribution to original knowledge, it is more to do with claiming a space and status for the kinds of embodied knowing and understanding about difference and diversity that members of minority groups experience on a daily basis, but which are so often disregarded in the policies and practices of mainstream education, when they should be recognised and valued. The research was not about answers but about finding the right questions. I have come to see that the important questions which should be central to educa-tional research are not really about the what, why or how of the issues at all, but more about the who. If my thesis makes a contri-bution at all, it is to all the people who participated in its develop-ment – and that is why it matters.

Why does it matter – to me?

About a year after I first registered for the MPhil/PhD, I attended a research workshop at the university of which the college where I worked was an associate. The other participants were mostly full-time PhD students and their supervisors, the majority of them funded by a whole range of councils, companies and other institutions to work on large, ongoing projects, mostly in the natural sciences. I remember feeling like a fish out of water and receiving surprised responses when I confessed that I was a part-time student and doing a full-time job at the same time, that my supervisor was at a University almost 200 miles away and that I was paying a good proportion of the fees myself. A sure recipe for failure, by all accounts.

I had a long and interesting conversation with one of the other participants at the workshop who was, I think, impressed by my capacity to place hope over experience. She was well into her full-time PhD, which was part of a huge project in biological sciences. She told me how bored she was with the work she was doing, and how she was only hoping to gain her doctorate so that she could qualify for university posts. I remember feeling surprised that she could be bored by doing research; I don't think I felt bored at any stage throughout the whole process of the PhD. I may have felt confused, worried, frustrated, exhausted and a whole gamut of other emotions, but my interest – indeed fascination – for the work I was doing grew steadily as the years went on. I found the reading, writing and talking about the issues and ideas utterly compelling, and I still do.

I began the PhD with no professional ambitions whatever – indeed, in the job I held at the time, there was no career enhancement to be gained from attaining a doctorate. My motivation at the start was entirely personal: to understand a problem which had bothered me for some years and which caused me considerable discomfort as a human being as well as a teacher. I have often wondered why it should have bothered me so much; perhaps it goes back to some personal sense of injustice that I have carried since I was a child, though I am not sure that causality could ever be established, or indeed works, in such a simple and sequential way as that suggests.

Something I am more sure about is the self-awareness and self-confidence I have gained from completing the PhD – and it was not until the final stages that I really believed I would do it. My research also helped me to bring meaning to my own somewhat fractured personal narrative; my childhood experiences in a small rural primary school and community, the years in Africa so different and vibrant and then so abruptly cut short, and then the – at times – confusing and troubling years in primary teaching and teacher training in England. This is how I described my early views on success in my autobiographical introduction:

> One of the key factors which, from my initial reflections on the classrooms I have inhabited, seemed to mediate success is the extent to which links can be made between and across the various contexts which both the teachers and learners inhabit, both in school and in the community. A sense of belonging is essential, whether to a Northumbrian primary school, a West African village, or a Pakistani social network ... More than ever, I have come to see that teaching cannot be a process of transferring knowledge from the 'teacher' to the 'taught', unless the 'taught' agree for it to be so.

I see much more clearly now that I was primarily writing about and for myself. In some ways, working on the PhD was a search for that sense of belonging which I had experienced as a child in a small school and community, and then later in the sunshine and hot colours of Sierra Leone. Perhaps this need to belong – to go back to Shirley Brice Heath once again – was my 'experiential, embodied knowledge', which I brought to the research and had to learn to theorise in order to discover what, for me, was wrong in the classrooms in which I subsequently found myself.

There have, of course, been professional benefits to completing, or – more accurately – carrying out the PhD. I believe that my expertise has grown in different ways, and I can now speak with greater weight and authority in the academic areas in which I work. Perhaps the greatest professional – and personal – benefit has been finding what Mishler (1990) describes as a 'community of scholars', a social network of people who share similar professional experiences and viewpoints on what should be regarded as the important issues in education and research.

Partly on the strength of the doctorate, I did get a new job and have moved to a professional context where I have much greater opportunity to pursue my research and writing interests. I understand

and can articulate my own approaches to teaching much more fully and confidently, and see more than ever the vital links between teaching and research. I am a much better writer now than I was when I started. Indeed, while I was working on the PhD, particularly doing the writing, I felt as if I gained authority and power to speak to the students I was teaching about the struggles of expressing ideas in words.

I believe it is essential to strive for simple language, no matter how complex the ideas, to avoid obfuscation and unnecessary jargon, always to write about educational research rooted in the ongoing human experiences of teaching and learning. This does not by any means represent an attack on theory – a theory-less approach to teaching and learning will always be sterile and usually be dangerous. What is needed in any educational context is a dynamic interaction between theory or theorising and practice, a process sometimes called praxis. When I wrote 'the book of the thesis' (Conteh, 2003), my first concern was to produce a text that was explicitly grounded in a sound theoretical framework, and which also offered practical strategies and approaches to teachers and ITT students to enhance their confidence in working with bilingual learners. When students and teachers comment on how clear they find the writing in the book, I feel great satisfaction. When they say they have enjoyed reading it, I am delighted.

Why does it matter – to the other participants in the research?

In writing the PhD, I wanted to find ways to show the active participation of the children, their parents and their teachers in the processes of education I was studying. The words I recorded belong to them, and so should the voices with which they are articulated. I read Cameron *et al.* (1992) and identified strongly with their call for research with (rather than on and for) the researched. I now see that I could have been more creative in seeking ways for the 'participants' to voice their own concerns in their own ways in the writing, to achieve the '*vraisemblance*' that Atkinson (1990) writes about, placing the implied reader in the role of 'first-hand witness' without my well-meaning interventions.

The contradictions faced by the children, teachers and parents in their daily encounters with difference and diversity in education, and the consequences of these for the children's success in school, were the mainspring and substance of the study. Because of my socio-economic and educational background, my job and – mostly – the colour of my skin, I am largely immune from the struggles which these encounters represent in the contexts I researched. I knew this dimly at the start, but I know it far more deeply and powerfully now.

If I did the project again, I would pursue the life history approach, which emerged in the interviews with the parents and some of the teachers, more diligently and confidently. Perhaps this would have led to different forms of writing and presentation in the final thesis; it has certainly led me at this point to a strong commitment to avoid unquestioning acceptance of traditional and conventional academic forms in my future writing, and to seek to break down hierarchical distinctions between researcher and researched in my future work.

But, this said, does the research really matter to the other participants? The four children who were at the centre of the whole enterprise have now completed their GCSEs and are moving on optimistically to various educational pursuits. Whether they can still be described as successful is probably the substance of another PhD project. I am still in occasional contact with three of them and, whenever I see them, they usually mention something about the times when I visited their classrooms and homes, and the things we talked about. They were delighted to receive copies of the book about the research when it came out.

They are all pleasant and articulate young people, no different from many others growing up in England today. The issues which have affected their opportunities so far, and will go on affecting them, are not substantially different from when I first met them as eight-year-olds in their Year 3 classroom, though perhaps they have been brought into sharper relief by recent global and local events. In some ways, I am sure, their awareness of themselves was raised by their involvement in the study, and this is something they still carry with them. It matters for other students like them that their experiences as young bilingual learners in mainstream classrooms were recorded, that these records have contributed in a small way to the growing body of research into diversity in schools in England and so the awareness of the importance of the issues addressed continues to grow.

Moving to the next layer, does it matter to the parents? Again, I still have limited contact with some of them. As far as I can see, they are still wholly committed to supporting their children's education, and no doubt still weighed down by the problems they have always encountered in bridging the gaps between family, community and mainstream schools, dealing with the resulting pressures with patience and perhaps – by now – resignation.

At this level, the research has probably made no difference to them at all, as it has not led to any changes in policy or practice. But, perhaps the memory that someone took an interest in them and spent time talking to them about their children – however briefly – helps them to feel that there is a purpose to their efforts. Perhaps it has added in small ways to their self-confidence in seeking to help their children to succeed. The only practical outcome I know about is that one of the mothers, partly as a result of our long conversations about the ways she worked with her children at home, felt confident enough to take on a job for a few hours a week as a support assistant in a school. But because of illness in the family, she was unable to keep it on for long.

For the teachers directly involved in the research, the outcomes were possibly even more diffuse. Janet and Sandra still work together, and I meet them from time to time. They work on with boundless patience and awesome attention to detail, but also with a growing sense of disillusion about national and local responses to the problems they face. They still have no real support from their normal professional contexts and contacts in mediating the fluid, ever changing demands of the daily lives of the children they teach and the community in which they work. Perhaps it boosted their self-esteem to have their classroom conversations recorded and analysed, and may have led them to think a little more positively and critically about their work. Or it may just have been a source of irritation that they prefer to forget. I prefer to think it was the former.

Why does it matter – to education?

The end of my PhD project coincided with a period of some turmoil in Bradford – though I don't think these events were linked. In education in the city, the huge re-organisation of the system from a three-tier to a two-tier one was coming to an end, and there was soon to be a correspondingly great overhaul of the management, with the appointment of a privatised company to take over key roles and reform the way things were done in the authority, in order to meet stringent targets. In the city, racial tension and unrest came to a head in July 2001 with riots, sparked off by clashes between BNP supporters and local Asian youths. Then, after September 11, 2001, cataclysmic events in the US were to have profound global and local repercussions, which have still to run their course.

I think if I were starting the project today, the ways in which I could do it would be very different. I might find it a lot harder to secure the free and generous access to classrooms and homes which I enjoyed in the late 1990s. The divisions between home and school might emerge as even wider and more difficult to bridge. I think it would probably become a relentlessly depressing and demoralising project to see to its conclusions.

But that is one viewpoint on the situation, and not the one I choose to allow to occupy my gaze for too long. One effect of the seismic global shifts of recent years, I believe, has been to bring issues of diversity and equality much more to the attention of the 'ethnic majority', who may in the past have chosen to ignore them in the hope that they would go away.

There is still a very long way to go, but I believe there is cause to be optimistic when initiatives to explore diversity and equality are popping up everywhere around us, supported – albeit misguidedly at times – by central and local government. More hopeful signs, perhaps, are to be found in the growing number of small, often voluntary activities happening in cities like Bradford. They illustrate the growing sense of empowerment – often fired by anger – of those to whom dealing with issues of diversity and difference is part of the daily texture of life.

One of the most positive signs in recent times, I think, is the growing number of ethnic minority individuals and groups becoming active and seeking their own ways of entering the debates. For example, I have been involved over the past few years with a voluntary association in Bradford in which bilingual teachers, through complementary classes, seek to raise primary children's confidence in using their own languages in their mainstream learning. This has given me a great sense of optimism.

While I was doing my PhD, I always hoped that at least one of the teachers in the study would be bilingual, in order to reflect a viewpoint about which I could not say anything. As it turned out, none were, and I could do nothing about it, given the nature of the research. But ever-increasing anecdotal evidence, and a small research project which I have just completed, continues to feed my imagination about the important roles which bilingual teachers from ethnic minority communities can play in mediating the worlds of home and school and improving access to the classroom interactions which are the crucible for successful learning for bilingual children. This is a fruitful and important area for future research.

The collusion continues

I now work in a University Department of Educational Studies, where I have all the privileges (as well as the civilised pressures) of a well-supported academic. The campus is usually calm and beautiful. At times I sit in my room, looking out of the window at the mature trees round the lake and listening to the ducks and geese as they go placidly about their watery activities. It can feel as if the stresses and strains involved in striving for equality and diversity are a million miles away. But, of course, this is not true – they are right there, and the need for collusion is just as vital.

I teach a module entitled *Culture, Language and Young Learners* to MA students, and recently I invited one of the bilingual teachers from our voluntary association to talk to my group. She is a qualified primary teacher, a Bangla speaker who came, at the age of five, to England from Bangladesh with her mother and older sister about twenty years ago. They came to join her father who had been here for some time, working to support his family. Shila spoke to the students about her memories of the sudden cold when, as a small child, she stepped off the plane with her mother and met the father who was, at the time, a stranger to her.

Two days later, her father took her by the hand to the school in Bradford in which she was to be enrolled. She talked about seeing a large white woman approach her, and how she was reassured by her smile. Then her father put her hand in the hand of the teacher, literally as well as metaphorically handing his young daughter over to strangers, and Shila was led away to her classroom. There she encountered many children who, like her, spoke a language different from English, but she was surprised to find that she could not understand them, not realising that they were speaking Punjabi.

Soon a small boy came to sit beside her and said in Bangla, *'Zebla teachare thumar naam khoyebla khoiyo 'yes miss"* (When you hear the teacher say your name, say 'yes miss'). Shila followed his instructions and so quickly overcame the first hurdle to being accepted in her new class. Then the boy disappeared from Shila's view into the busy classroom.

At playtime, she followed all the other children into the cold, noisy playground and decided to seek out her mentor and fellow Bangla-speaker. Spotting him in the distance, she ran towards him excitedly. His response was not what she expected. 'Don't stand with me,' he said, in the language they shared, 'and don't speak to me in Bangla any more'. And he ran off, anxious not to be identified as a speaker of the language that would mark him out as different from all the other children energetically playing around him.

The MA students were entranced by Shila's story, but slightly puzzled. With the help of a map, she explained the historical and political tensions between Bangladesh and Pakistan, divided from India by partition in 1947, and later from each other by violent bloodshed.

Listening to Shila and appreciating the nature and power of the collusion shown by that little boy in her class so many years ago, I realised how her story connected with mine. Just at the time she was learning about what it meant to be a bilingual child in a Bradford school, I was beginning my time there as a teacher and teacher-trainer. In another classroom not far from hers, I was just about to meet another Bangla-speaking child, Mushaq, whom I introduced in Chapter One – another child from Bangladesh whose self-confidence and awareness were to help him succeed in a strange new education system, just as Shila's did her.

When the seminar was over, Shila and I went for a walk round the campus. She delighted in the colours of the autumn leaves, and in her opportunity to be in such a prestigious setting. We went into the library, and she asked to look at the language books. There, on the shelves, she immediately spotted a set of old, hardbacked Bengali language grammar and poetry books, which had probably not left the library for years. When I offered to borrow them for her, Shila was delighted. So was I – I imagined her and her siblings and perhaps their father, in their home in Bradford, poring over the books from the University library. As we walked back over the walkway from the library to the car park, Shila carried her borrowed books and talked of her anticipated pleasure in showing them to her family. I listened and thought about Bateson's 'patterns that connect'. I felt pleased at being party to another small act of collusion, and – suddenly – full of hope for the future.

11

In search of some answers: analysing the stories and reflections on policy

Chris Kearney

The point to make is not whether biographical coherence is an illusion or a reality. Rather what must be established is how individuals give coherence to their lives when they write or talk self-auto-biographies. The source of this coherence, the narratives that lie behind them, and the larger ideologies that structure them must be uncovered. Denzin (1977)

Sorting the conversations – the first layer: the pattern that connects

It was at an early research meeting that Eve introduced us to Gregory Bateson's maxim that research is a quest for 'the pattern that connects'. So from my first interview with Aliki I was listening continually to the tapes, looking for patterns and themes. I was also looking for insights which challenged my own views. By the time I analysed my first three interviews in 1997, which later became the 'Deep Excavations' article, I had begun to draw out some general patterns.

- Patterns of family settlement – rural to urban
- Economically supported by family and community

- Conceptions of identity as fluid and mobile
- A strong sense of history and affiliation with heritage cultures
- Ambivalence and questioning of value systems of the heritage culture and wider society
- Looking outside community for life partners
- Influence of the mass media on sense of identity
- Strong influence of peer group,as a support network
- Frequent visits to homeland
- An ambivalent attitude to living in the homeland
- An enjoyment of schooling and learning but no ostensible examples of how this connected to daily lives
- Liberal, tolerant values and a critical outlook generally associated with aspects of a Western, liberal humanist education
- Identification with other oppressed or marginalised groups.

This was interesting but not very systematic. It needed refinement. I also realised that I needed to find an analytical tool with which I could investigate the complexity and contradiction embodied here. In short, I needed a map of the syncretic processes. I also had to relate my findings to my theoretical reading of identity. A by-product of the methodology chapter was that I was able to sort my theoretical readings on identity into four broad categories and locate myself within the arguments. This in turn enabled me to identify the gaps which I hoped to address in my own work. It also underlined the need for discovering an analytical tool sophisticated enough to capture pattern and avoid overgeneralisation and stereotype.

In my final version of the 'literature chapter', I describe the four broad categories of identity as follows:

> In summary the debate concerning the self rages in many academic areas, each with a different approach. In this chapter I have tried to isolate and analyse four main approaches, which affect our work as teachers.

- *The enlightenment concept* of a self-contained individual ack-nowledged that we experience reality in a unique body which has a certain degree of continuity. This released people from the notion of a natural order of things. It undermined the oppressive nature of the philosophy Great Chain of Being (ie that we occupy a preordained position in the world) with its deeply hierarchical and entrenched view of power. What it didn't account for was the social nature of identity

- *The social models of identity* attempted to address the problems of the nature of identity and in many cases over-estimated the social nature of identity. The more negative forces worked against a recognition of the individual's ethical responsibility for their own actions or their part in the con-struction of their own identity

- *Postmodernist models of identity:* This creative notion has been taken up by the postmodernists who have posited a creative and constantly changing view of self as we respond to rapid social and technological changes. However, they under-estimate the force of cultural memory and the need for a co-herent and continuous self

- *Social psychologists* have posited theories of 'storied' identities by which we make sense of our past life and the pre-sent by constantly updating our narratives to produce coherent narratives of self.

... what is missing from the research is any systematic cross cul-tural study which seeks to analyse how these complex construc-tions of identity are achieved in second generation settlers, who have reached adulthood and have integrated the various com-peting forces acting upon them in a way which is rare in adoles-cents

Transcribing the tapes

Having clarified this aspect, I set about refining the patterns that connect. Up to this point, I had not fully transcribed the tapes but only selected excerpts. I was fortunate those episodes turned out to be pivotal examples for me. There was still much to do. So it began gradually for me. And slowly. Transcribing.

Anyone who has engaged in this kind of work knows that, in its own way, it is as long, dull and tedious as a slow night-shift in a factory. It is especially dull if you type as slowly as I do. That's why mine are handwritten. I bought several spiral bound Quarto notebooks from Paperchase. The pages were ruled into tiny squares. I chose squared paper in case I needed to draw tables and charts. I decided to transcribe the stories onto one side of the paper, leaving the facing page blank for comments or analysis. It was a job I had studiously avoided and I made all kinds of excuses to Eve for my procrastination. However, I did have a system. After I had transcribed each interview, I read them through looking for patterns and thinking of what they told me about the construction of their individual identities.

Laborious as it is, I'm glad I did it myself. There are several benefits. Most importantly, the voices echo in your head with all the richness of their individual tone and timbre. Even at this distance when I read their words, I can evoke their distinctive voices. In the process I became sensitive to delicate nuances of meaning. It reminded me that speech conveys a great deal of its semantic weight through music and that we ignore this at our peril. Secondly you can hear the patterns. I knew the stories so well after the sixth or seventh listen that making comparisons between the narratives became much easier. I also had the written versions for quick cross-referencing. Rewinding tapes is slow.

When looking for patterns and common themes, I was pleased that my closer reading confirmed my original intuitions. I was also pleased that, when I presented my findings to students or at conferences, there were always people who would come to me at the end of the session to tell me how closely the stories and my analyses coincided with their own experiences. They also made further observations and asked searching questions which helped me to refine what I was doing. In this process I now reconfigured my initial observations in a more patterned and systematic way. The second point I make here is that I needed to keep their own individuality alive if my representation was to remain true and, here, I was very much influenced by Mark Freeman in *Rewriting the Self; History, Memory, Narrative*. His work helped me arrive at a more systematic analysis of the patterns. Here is how I describe it in the thesis:

> Freeman (1993:29) reminds us
>
> Memory, therefore, which often has to do not merely with recounting the past, but making sense of it – from 'above' as it were– is an interpretive act the end of which is an enlarged understanding of the self

After quoting Freeman, I continue:

> Although this chapter concentrates on the content of their self narratives, embedded within the anecdotes are their own well articulated and evaluative arguments. Self narrative is always about point of view. This is what makes it such a rich resource. The layers of context, action and evaluation, reflection, philosophy and standpoint are contained within the attractive, familiar, ordinary and accessible framework of story.
>
> To analyse the common patterns in the narratives I shall be organising the work thematically. I present them as sets of the relationships. I have chosen to begin with the family, which is generally where the most intimate and formative relationships occur, and worked outwards in what I consider are widening spheres of influence.

I reached this point early in 2000 but I didn't finish transcribing the tapes or begin writing this section up until my study leave period from October to December and I'll come back to that later.

The second layer: Bakhtin's triad

The more closely I listened and looked at the transcripts I had completed, the more I saw other patterns. There was certainly a great deal of pain in these stories, even if the tone seemed more optimistic and at times almost jokey. I also noticed that they were all managing immense competing and contradictory forces and attempting to sort out riddles and dilemmas. It was interesting to observe that these well-balanced, articulate and gregarious individuals were carrying such dark emotional undertow. I glimpsed all this beneath the surface, but as yet could find no tools to draw it out and analyse it.

It was around this time that I had been reading a great deal about narrative analysis: Clandenin and Connolly (2000), Cortazzi (1993) and Reissman (1993). Increasingly I was drawn to the work of Social Psychologists and the centrality of narrative in their theories. This provided a strong link to the works on literature related to culture and memory, which I had been reading since early 1997.

The breakthrough came from a book on Bakhtin written by Morson and Emerson (1990), two scholars whom I had admired when I working on my MA. In a chapter entitled 'Psychology' I found something of enormous help to me. They describe an early work in which Bakhtin had been discussing how characters develop in the 19th century novel and talks of individuals having three dimensions to their 'identity'.

Others for self: how other people affect our sense of our self

Self for others: how we modify our behaviour in presenting ourselves to others

Self for self: how the process feels from the inside

Having rejected the predominant tools of narrative analysis such as conversation analysis and discourse analysis, it seemed that I had stumbled across something which might work. Hesitantly I tried it out in pencil. Coding their stories. Sorting them into categories. As their narratives were densely packed, it didn't seem to work. I opted for a 'best fit' approach. This seemed to work. After playing with this for a while, I decided I would try to plot them onto a grid. It consisted of three columns headed, 'others for self', 'self for others' and 'self for self' respectively. The first two columns, 'others for self' and 'self for others', related to outside influences upon their identity. The third aspect, 'self for self' concerned their internal life.

Using the grid enabled me to study the interplay among the different aspects. To make this manageable I had to summarise each episode. It was then that I realised that the different episodes had a certain attitude or state of mind attached to them; for example *influence, ambivalence or discomfort*. This was the beginning of my coding process. What was emerging even at this stage was a clearer picture of how these young adults were managing the disparate influences upon them into a coherent sense of self. It was not just a matter of slipping in and out of identities. They were reworking memories in critical and analytical ways. There were common patterns to this and the key to it all seemed to be narrative.

I had the opportunity of trying these observations out at the Ethnography Forum at the University of Pennsylvania in Philadelphia in 1999. It was another cold visit to an American city. Even in March, the piles of snow at the edge of the sidewalk were several feet high. The cold contrasted dramatically with the warm atmosphere of the conference itself. People were friendly and there were fascinating and illuminating talks, discussions and presentations. The conference's particular appeal to me is that delegates represent a rich variety of cultural heritages. Between the sessions there was a chance to talk with interesting people from all over the world, some of whom were studying at Penn, who were working in a variety of contexts. Yet there was also a common sense of purpose and commitment. Again several people expressed genuine interest in my presentation, made valuable suggestions and inspired me to continue. The questions led me to be clearer and more specific about my categories. On returning to England I intended to refine them further.

Out of time: observations on policy

However, when I returned to England I was distracted temporarily from this work. There were plans afoot for a revision of the National Curriculum. Here was a great opportunity to effect significant change and work out a curriculum which could, at its heart, recognise the diverse reality of contemporary Britain. The recent Macpherson enquiry into the murder of Stephen Lawrence (1999) had raised serious issues concerning policing and social policy. It also had implications in terms of culture, identity and education. However, the signs for radical change were not good. David Blunkett 's proposals for Curriculum 2000 contained few changes. In response to the Lawrence inquiry the need for courses in citizenship were emphasised. This is a controversial area since official definitions sidestep notions of complex identity and are scarcely different in substance from the assimilationist approaches of the 1960s and 1970s.

A sensitive and well researched report by a committee chaired by Ken Robinson and commissioned by David Blunkett himself was shelved. The report entitled *All Our Futures: Creativity, Culture and the Curriculum* describes the complexity of issues of culture and identity in modern Britain. Not only does it make workable recommendations, it details how a policy may be implemented. In short, it provided a workable alternative to the outmoded National Curriculum. It also embodied notions of complex identities which were much more closely aligned to my own research. I was moved to write something (Kearney, 2000). For my argument in this article, I critiqued, among other things, the proposals for the new curriculum. The finished piece formed the basis of my concluding chapter and only needed slight revision by the time I presented my thesis to Senate House nine months later.

The final straight

From March 2000 onwards I worked on various aspects of my thesis. By that time I had completed my final interview. Following a predictable routine, I put in a proposal to the ATEE 2000 conference which was to be held in Barcelona in August. I decided to present a paper where I analysed the responses of my second three participants, much on the lines I had followed for 'Deep Excavations'. There was a significant difference between the two groups. Whereas my first group had all been born in Britain, the others had arrived later.

My was a refugee from Vietnam (one of the Boat People) and was six years old when she made her perilous journey. Olgun was a Turkish Cypriot who was eleven when he arrived to stay with relatives in Charlton. Michael was ten when he was reunited with his parents who had left Dominica for England when he was about five years old. I found that they were subtly different and, although they had similar dilemmas concerning their identity, they had much closer allegiances with their homeland, having lived there for a significant period. They also have a keener awareness of the colonial struggles, having tasted them at first hand in all their subtlety and brutality.

In contrast to the conferences in the US, August in Barcelona was stifling and humid. I presented my paper in a large, dark and mercifully cool ancient hall in the University. I met several people on that visit who asked me searching questions about my approach. Some of them have remained close colleagues. The effect was to galvanise my thoughts and, now I had all the information I intended to use, I could begin to see the narrative shape of the thesis as a whole. I knew my argument and I was confident about my approach. I knew there was still much to do and that I needed a concentrated block of time to work upon it.

Study leave

My university granted me study leave in the Autumn Term of 2000 and it was the best thing to happen at that stage. It was a peculiar experience. Having always worked with some structure to my day which was imposed by necessity, the freedom and responsibility of setting my own timetable was stranger than I had anticipated. The time went quickly. I still had masses of transcribing to do and the three 'analysis' chapters to write, virtually from scratch. The transcribing was intense and eerie. It was also painfully slow. In my notebook I explode regularly with exasperation and self-pity: 'Transcribing is such a bloody chore. It takes forever, gives me stiff fingers and a headache. In more senses than one'. By the third week I was panicking that I still hadn't completed the transcriptions. I was anxious that I might run out of time. In retrospect I needn't have worried.

I kept to my old routine. In the mornings I would rise early and get on with transcriptions until about half past ten. Then I would work on coding the interviews for the grids. In the afternoons I would go into the libraries. In this final stage it tended to be the British Library and I can tell by the notebooks that the emphasis was on narrative and memory. Amongst many others I was reading Suzanne Langer (1941), Clandenin and Connolly (1994, 2000), Gergen (1989, 1994), Rosenwald and Ochburg (1992). All helped immensely in making sense of stories and the self. It was an exciting period. I was also refining the categories. Patterns were beginning to emerge.

Patterns that connect (continued)

Once I had completed my transcriptions, I realised that I must now set to work on the analysis chapters in earnest. I was writing against the clock. I had arranged with Eve that I would send my first draft of each chapter to her for comment as soon as it was complete. The patterns that connect were fairly straightforward, since I would follow the structure of the list. I decided that not only would I select parts of their narratives which were similar for each section, but also demonstrate that beneath this similarity were subtle individual differences.

The writing came very easily. The voices were fresh in my head. I followed my list doggedly and systematically. As I wrote one anecdote, I would be reminded of a similar anecdote from another person. Juxtaposing them brought out subtle differences, which in turn led to further patterns. It did not take me as long as I had anticipated to complete the chapter. In fact most of the writing at this stage came effortlessly and fluently. I knew where I was going and what I wanted to say, so the rest was just happy discovery on the journey. Most of the time I was orchestrating their voices in a way that I hoped would do justice to the complexity of their stories. It was then that I realised that the first part of the analysis should begin with more coherent pictures of them. It was at that point I decided I would use an amalgam of two papers: 'Deep Excavations' (1998) and the one presented to the Barcelona conference. It would become a separate introductory chapter. I sent these two chapters to Eve and began on my next chapter almost immediately.

By this time, I was fully absorbed in the writing and spent many days alone at the computer. Very much in my own head. Abstract notions running and running. I felt removed. I was in a strange place. It was not an altogether unpleasant experience. In many ways it was peaceful and meditative. But it was a lonely place. For many years I had harboured a romantic view of a writer's life. This experience punctured that dream. Up until this point my work on the thesis had been part of an ongoing dialogue with others. Thanks to our supervisor, it was not an isolated or isolating experience. These last few miles I had to do alone. It was a strange time.

Back to Bakhtin

Where Freud describes a conflict between the conscious and the unconscious. Voloshinov (in the 1920s) and Bakhtin in the 1920s and 1930s) describe a complex dialogue among the numerous, diverse, socially heteroglot voices present in inner speech.

> Basically their contention is that thinkers turn to an unconscious
> when they have an extraordinarily impoverished idea of conscious-
> ness. As Bakhtin was to write in the early 1960s in his notes for re-
> working the Dostoevsky book, 'consciousness is much more terrify-
> ing than any unconscious complexes' (Morson and Emerson, 1990:
> 175)

There will always be parts of your thesis which you are less happy
with than others. This part was it for me. Not because I think I was
on the wrong track here. Quite the reverse. I just don't think I had
the time to elaborate and refine it enough. The idea is central to my
understanding of identity. It links the individual to the social and
brings them into a dialectical relationship with each other. So it
links with Vygotsky's thinking closely and, more obviously, Bakhtin's
as well. Reading Randall's (1995) view of identity creation confirmed
for me that the grid would help unriddle this problem. He says:

> I propose that if the concept of story applies to life at all, that the
> application is in relation to one or other or some combination of
> four possible levels: existence, experience, expression and impres-
> sion (page 48)

He summarises them as:

> Existence: the outside story
> Experience: the inside story
> Expression: the inside-out story
> Impression: the outside-in story

I felt that the grids would chart these interrelationships well. I knew
I would have to limit this analysis to make it manageable. I thought
three excerpts would be enough. I chose them carefully; one each
from Aliki, Asif and Michael. In my view they would have to consist
of major turning points in their narrative leading to some kind of
epiphany, if they were going to illustrate how they maintain a coherent sense of identity. I also chose episodes which showed the difficulty and dilemmas they faced in the process which they were
resolving through narrative. I then engaged in a close textual
analysis of the three episodes, giving context and background. The
grids I produced demonstrated the ebb and flow between the different levels; perspectives from the inside and the outside. I also
noted in looking at more general patterns that the narrative

sequences tended to move from dealing with outside influences to the internal thoughts and resolutions of problems or dilemmas. There was always some kind of conflict which was ultimately resolved internally. In short it demonstrated clearly how they wove their contradictions into a coherent sense of self by continually reworking their memories of their lives through narrative. It was a significant finding, but I still think that there is a mystery at the heart of it which continues to elude me. Time constraints forced me to abandon this particular problem and move on. I spent about a week writing it up and sent my draft to Eve for comment.

The third layer: the question of voice

While I was examining the final story, another level occurred to me. The story I analysed was Michael's. He was a young man from Dominica and he told of a serious assault he had endured as a teenager at the hands of racists in Canning Town. His story was structured and poetic with unmistakeable Caribbean cadences. At the end of October in my journal entry, just following my complaint against transcribing, I note:

> Transcribing is however totally necessary. It does enable me to get deep inside the interview. Michael's one is interesting. His rhetorical style is consistent throughout. It's not really a storyteller's either but more of a preacher's. It is repetitive often to the point of exhaustion. But it always comes back to the same theme via a slightly different route.

A few things started to come together at this point. I had been interested for some time in what persisted when people crossed boundaries and frontiers and how it persisted. In Chapter Five I have noted how this problem occurred to me as early as Easter 1996. James Clifford had also raised that issue and linked it to memory. Then I read *Angela's Ashes* which was written by a man in his sixties who had only spent a short period of his life in Ireland. In it I recognised idioms and ways of speaking that were similar to the way my mother spoke when I was young. My mother had never visited Ireland at that point. In fact it was her grandparents who had come over from Ireland and settled in Leeds. The book also refers to several lesser-known Irish songs which I knew. Both the words and the tunes came back to me while reading it. It led me to begin to investigate voice as a key to this problem.

At the time I was reading Gee's work on Discourse (1989, 1991, 1992, 1996) and Hymes' (1996) close linguistic analysis of Native American patterns of storytelling. Drawing on earlier work by Labov, Hymes transcribes spoken language as poetry with lines and stanzas. Once I tried this I realised that, not only did it capture Michael's distinctive rhythms and cadences, it also revealed the powerful symmetrical architecture of his narrative style. This led me back to Labov's stories from teenagers in Harlem in the late 1960s, collected by Jerome Robbins his black researcher (Labov, 1972a and b). To my astonishment, there were distinct similarities between Michael's story and those of the black teenagers from Labov's study. Labov's analyses also seemed to fit. More work needs to be done in this area but I felt that it was a productive direction which needed to be included in the thesis.

A final word

The chapter on voice was a really wonderful writing experience for me. It came as a whole chapter at two or three sittings. I was 'on a roll'. I scarcely had to revise the compositional elements. It said what I wanted it to say. Now the transcriptional elements. They were a different matter. I find the niceties of prescriptive grammar a bit of a nightmare. Some of my idiosyncratic ways of expressing myself are through choice. I can be deliberately wilful with the English language when I want. I like verbless sentences. For the rest, I need help and have been fortunate enough to have critical readers who are sensitive to my style. Eve helped me to get it into shape for the viva and I presented the thesis to the University in 2001. I had met my own deadline and I had the viva in June.

Because I had presented the work continually to many audiences and because sections of it were published as conference papers or were published in journals, the viva was quite enjoyable. It was a discussion of interesting issues arising from it rather than a defence of my thesis in the traditional mode. Moreover, I realised that, in the course of writing it, I had changed. I had been able to work through ideas which were important to me on many levels. They connected at a deep level with my own life, but they also linked with my own particular political standpoint. In her book, *My Invented Country* Isabelle Allende talks about her own strong longing to belong to a community, yet at the same time jealously guarding her right to raise uncomfortable questions which upset members of that community. Particularly when she is moved by some injustice or intolerance to speak or write. It's a dilemma I can recognise. It permeates my work. It is also a dilemma of all six people I spoke to.

But what takes this dilemma far beyond the personal is that it is central to the political struggles emerging through the so-called New World Order. It is a growing dilemma in a world where communities are being radically altered and global economic systems exacerbate injustice. We now live in a world where poverty spirals and the poor are subjected to the anarchy of a market which is not interested in ethical niceties. It is a system which can easily ignore the rise of all kinds of slavery and approve of factories being run without any regulation, decent pay or protection for workers. It is an approach which can remain impervious to the horror of bitter conflicts between different communities of ethnicity or religion or both. Such communities tend to be poor and either non-white or from the former Soviet bloc.

On the other hand the rich are feted and encouraged to abuse their power and wallow in the luxury afforded by a blizzard of money, power and privilege blowing in their direction from the poorest corners of the earth. In this vision of the world, if you are not greedy and self-seeking you are condemned as naive and stupid. National governments appear indifferent or powerless to stem this tide. At the centre of this study is the question of who, or what, controls and defines the identity of individuals and social groups, nations and cultures. This is as much a political as an intellectual formulation, for it involves a critical reassessment of the practice of globalism.

In this scenario, where we stand and who we really are are the dilemmas we need to resolve. Memories are long. That is why the issue of identity has become so prominent in the intellectual life of the West. It is a mistake for the rich to think that history is dead. As we have seen in the Balkans, old wounds rarely heal. Centuries pass. We do not forget, let alone forgive. A new form of identity politics is needed to bring people together without ignoring the past. It is made all the more urgent by the fact that, in the past fifteen years, we have seen the rise of gangsterism as a major factor in the global economy and a dramatic increase worldwide in trafficking of arms, drugs and human beings across borders. The people involved are driven by poverty to make desperate, brutal and even fatal choices. Simultaneously, at a local level, identities are often hardening into the most basic and conservative variants.

However, if I have learned anything, it is that certain elements of identity are particularly resilient when people cross borders. I have also learned that they are, paradoxically, also open to outside influences. Both the continuity and the changes are borne by stories, art, music, language and other ways of expressing ourselves. I also realise that human beings are peculiarly effective in preventing themselves from going mad, even in extreme conditions, by narrating their histories and identities, constantly weaving the past with the present. Writing the thesis enabled me to find some, perhaps temporary, resolution of my own dilemmas. It enabled me to develop my voice and my confidence in this area. My profound thanks go to all who helped me on that journey. They helped me arrive at a fuller understanding of these complex and important issues. Also they have not diminished my hope. In these uneasy and uncertain days their courage has reinvigorated my optimism for the long run. My hope is that what I found out on the way may be of use to others. Of course, like any study that is personally important, it's a journey that never really ends.

12

Into the future:
towards a universal approach
to cultural bilingualism

Aura Mor-Sommerfeld

When I began this study, my aim was to examine young children's behaviour as they begin to develop literacy in a new language; I focused on the role of children's literature in this process. Because of my findings I argue that children develop a new type of relationship between their first language and the new one. Using the knowledge they have in the first language, and relying on their own theories regarding languages, books and scripts, children develop strategies in order to function in the new learnt language. This work examines this issue and analyses it in the context of L1 Hebrew and L1 Arabic children learning and developing English as a new-additional language in Israel.

This was the opening to the last chapter – the conclusion – of my thesis. Here I summarise some aspects of the study presented in this book, and deal with how one sets about writing such a chapter. Some ideas about writing a thesis, particularly in another language, are integrated in the text. In a way, this chapter reflects how the other chapters of this book were written – the personal aspects, professional development, and the topic, combining into a coherent summary of *what* and *how*.

But there is one small difference. A conclusion is a serious matter. This is evident in, among other things, how it is written. The language, for example, is more definite and expressions like *I may*, *this might* or *I guess* become statements: – *I argue*, *my arguments* or *I state*. This is more about the cognitive dimension (what) and less about feelings (how and why). In this last chapter, then, I focus more on the what – what should be written; what are/were my conclusions – and less on the how – how to write them – just as I did when I wrote the conclusion of my study, all those years ago.

The first dimension of this chapter summarises contextual conclusions deriving from my own research. The second considers their meaning and importance both for theory and for practice: research, policy and field. The two dimensions are interwoven, and together they form the infrastructure of my writing, again integrating text with context. The text means the conclusions derived from the process, referring to a specific research, parts of which are described in other chapters of this book; while context is provided by the conclusion chapter itself.

My comparative study investigated how two groups of young children from very different backgrounds develop literacy in English as a new language, with children's literature as the core of the curriculum. A critical view of ethnography suggests that one of its disadvantages may be a tendency to focus on the failure of a whole ethnic group in light of microethnographic studies in the classroom. The attitude of this study is absolutely different.

Although one of the groups presented has much lower socio-economic status in Israel than the others, the children in it succeeded just as well. The starting point of each group was very different, yet they all made a great deal of progress in the new language.

This ethnographic and ethnomethodological study has tried to observe and understand the participants as they act and negotiate in and between different situations during the learning process. When completing the work I could illustrate and define this as three interlocking triangles, namely:

▲ child, teacher, book

▲ language, literature, literacy

▲ English, Arabic, Hebrew.

The concluding chapter of my thesis summarises the three facets of each triangle thus:

> ...Through these triangles I have created the framework and set up the parameters of my work. Together they supply the *context* and establish the premise of the *text*... Examining these connections is one aspect of this discussion; applying the conclusions should be one of the goals...

> ...Any attempt to discuss them discretely would be difficult, since each group and each element within each group is connected to the other two groups and their components. Nevertheless, I find this procedure logical and challenging. I argue that it contributes to our understanding of how young children develop literacy in a new language.

The following chart represents the relationships and connections between the three triangles and their elements, showing how such connections develop in and into bilingualism. Assisted by the book and the teacher on the one hand, and the first language on the other, the child encounters literature in a new language. She/he then acquires and develops a new language which influences the first. This process causes and enables a mutual flow between the first and the new language. It presents a theory encapsulating the process of becoming bilingual as a culture. This occurs through new language development, and not just through social mobility or striking roots.

This model (page 170) currently has particular relevance to Israel (and possible to other places suffering conflict). The possibility of linking two first languages, in this case Arabic and Hebrew, is both

A cultural model for bilingualism

a process of learning

child

teacher   book
instruction   the world of the child
through books   *meets the world of*
                                 the book

in terms of: in terms of:

literature

literacy
creating language mosaic

language

(learning)

•

a new language (L2)
English

•

Arabic (L1)   •   Hebrew (L1)

•

child

linguistically and politically very attractive. The chart implies the existence of a dialogue not just between the new and the first language, but also between the languages in conflict, perhaps even through a third one. Such a dialogue can apply both to socio-political and to cognitive-cultural issues (the child, the person). In this context, although I refer to the socio-political issues in Israel, this could be a universal approach. Regarding the cognitive-cultural aspect, I find this an ultimately viable model.

There is more. In 1998 Ariel Dorfman, dramatist and publicist, published an article under the title 'If only we all spoke two languages'. He wrote: '... turning and making me into this hybrid creature who now uses both languages and writes a memoir in English and a play in Spanish as if it were the most ordinary thing to do'. This is exactly what I feel about bilingualism. Doesn't Dorfman's example ultimately represent this model?

Thoughts about this model and about other possibilities continue to preoccupy me. The urge to contribute to the field, both theoretically and practically, has remained. A few months after completing my thesis, I developed the original model as follows:

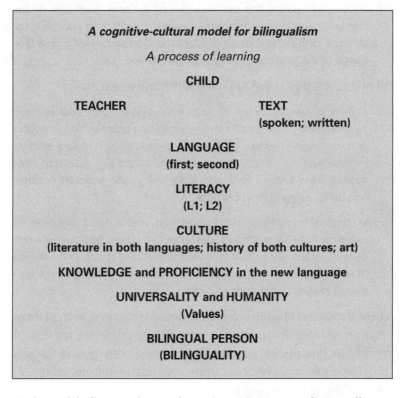

A cognitive-cultural model for bilingualism

A process of learning

CHILD

TEACHER   **TEXT**
                     (spoken; written)

LANGUAGE
(first; second)

LITERACY
(L1; L2)

CULTURE
(literature in both languages; history of both cultures; art)

KNOWLEDGE and PROFICIENCY in the new language

UNIVERSALITY and HUMANITY
(Values)

BILINGUAL PERSON
(BILINGUALITY)

Both models fit my odyssey through writing my work. By collocating ideas I have created this collusion of languages (my first and my other) in order to establish my own approach to the theory of language development. For me, this socio-linguistic research has become a personal study, an extended developmental process, both personal and professional.

As an educational study my work discusses possible implications of the findings, and offers strategies for their implementation in regard to *practice, politics* and *research*. All of them are concerned with L1 and L2 learning and development. In my thesis I wrote:

> The *practical* aspect of this study concerns *new/second* language learning and instruction, as well as first language literacy development. As regards learning a *new or second language*, it advocates the consistent use of children's literature to create a natural context, and to bring the cultural environment of the target language closer for the L2 learner by relying on the universal phenomenon of narrative. In terms of writing, *language mosaic* should be allowed and encouraged during the development of the new language. As for first language literacy, this work proposes a different approach for children with difficulties, and offers the introduction of a new language in the process of literacy development.

All of this is firmly linked to both politics and research.

> *Politics* is seen in terms of both *educational policy* and *political relationships* between different groups and communities. Allowing or encouraging the use of language mosaic should have a marked influence on the educational system, and might also extend to establishing new criteria for using it among young children in other countries, using different scripts.

> In regard to *political relationships*, it would be interesting to examine how far children's literature can create bridges between groups, especially groups in conflict, and how it opens the minds of young children taking their first steps in developing a new language to other languages and races.

These two issues obviously open the door for *research;* each of them requires individual attention. A new *ethnographic research* could investigate how the universal approach works with other languages and, hopefully, achieve better understanding of cultural bilingualism and bilingual development.

I concluded the epilogue to my work thus:

> Above all, this work is about young children. It discusses their literacy development, how they cope with a new language, and the role of children's literature in their learning process, but it is not just about languages, not just about literature or children's literature. It is about the children. It is they who have made the rest possible.

The road to a new universal approach to cultural bilingualism is opening.

Epilogue

The Authors

Jean: Most (existing?) research is individual, it's not about links with your community and collaborating and yet that's so powerful, because, all the going to conferences etc.... I wouldn't have done it on my own because I wouldn't have had the confidence...

Eve: It's also about believing that what you say matters and, if you're on your own, how can you do that? You need other people to tell you that...

Chris: Also, if you're part of a network, others see the development in your work, which you yourself miss. They say, 'Oh, that's really come on.' And you say, 'Has it really?'

Aura: For me, that was even more important. Coming all the way to London and seeing that it still matters...

For readers who prefer to begin at the end, we need to stress that that this book is not a conventional text about ethnography as a research methodology. Nor does it deal simply with the writing of an ethnographic study, as the first part of its title suggests. Rather, it is an honest and intimate account of all the joys and problems, fears and successes of actually doing the ethnographic work that informs the writing.

Throughout the book we question the notion of educational research as neutral and objective and argue for a recognition of personal experience as a starting-point. This view of knowledge means a realisation that our way of understanding the world changes as we experience new things; that knowledge is a continuous process of reflection rather than an objective reality (Kelly, 1955). We do not claim that knowledge is subjective; rather that we should be aware of our subjectivity and accept the limitations of our work. This approach carries its own terminology and we aim for 'trustworthiness' (Mishler, 1990) rather than 'validity'. The result is an exciting study; clear proof that PhDs do not have to be boring to be rigorous!

The metaphor of the PhD as a journey has often been used in our discussions together. Practically, all our studies have travelled around the world at various stages in their making (whether for conference presentations, supervision sessions or journal articles). Metaphorically, the synthesis of ideas and arguments in the final studies compared with early field-notes reveals the intellectual distance travelled by the authors over their years of work. We share the analogy of the PhD as an apprenticeship, a rite of passage. Along the way, we all learned what counts as research, how to present an argument, how to divide and section the work. Importantly, however, taking the path proposed in this book also leads to the cohesion needed in the final study; cohesion gained through constantly returning to the autobiographical chapter. In Jean's words: 'it is the voice that provides the cohesion; we need to trust the voice...'. However, the journey does not end with the PhD. Indeed, completing the study is an exercise, a pilot study for further work rather than an end in itself; it cannot be perfect, nor should it try to be. It is a beginning for the real work to come.

Journeys can be tedious if undertaken alone. Crucially, as ethnographers we have companions who are constantly present along the way. We hope in this book to have shown ways in which the principal aim of our research has been to give a voice to others less able to make their voices heard. In so doing, we have discovered what really matters to us and have been able to find our own voice. Thus, our work concerns the art of collusion with all those who accompany us on our way, and so we have chosen the sub-title to this book. We have colluded with our participants as under-represented communities, with our colleagues and other students with whom we have shared ideas, with our supervisors, with each other in our discussions on the book and finally, we hope, with you as its readers in gaining your own voice as you engage in and develop your work.

Bibliography

Alasuutari, P (1995) *Researching Culture: Qualitative Method and Cultural Studies* London: Sage

Ang, I (1994) On not Speaking Chinese: Postmodern Ethnicity and the Politics of Diaspora *New Formations*, 24 (Winter) pp 1-18

Apple, MW (1989) *Teachers and Texts: A Political Economy of Class and Gender Relations in Education* London: Routledge

Atkinson, P (1990) *The Ethnographic Imagination: Textual Constructions of Reality* London: Routledge

Au, KH (1980) Participant Structures in a Reading Lesson with Hawaiian Children: Analysis of a Culturally Appropriate Instructional Event *Anthropology and Education Quarterly*, 11(2) pp 115-152

Bakhtin, M (1981) *The Dialogic Imagination* Texas: University of Texas Press

Bakhtin, M (1984) *The Problems of Dostoevsky's Poetics* Manchester: Manchester University Press

Bakhtin, M (1986) *Speech Genres and Other Late Essays* Texas: University of Texas Press

Bateson, G (1979) *Mind and Nature* London: Wildwood House

Becker, HS (1986) *Doing Things Together* Evanston, IL: Northwestern University Press

Bentahila, A (1983) *Language Attitudes Among Arabic-French Bilinguals in Morocco* Clevedon: Multilingual Matters

Bialystok, E (1996) Metalinguistic Dimensions of Bilingual Language Proficiency in: Bialystok, E (ed) *Language Processing in Bilingual Children* Cambridge: Cambridge University Press, pp 113-140

Brecht, B *Die Auswanderung der Dichter. Gedichte 1914-1956.* Frankfurt am Main: Suhrkamp Verlag

Brecht, B (1976) *Poems 1913-1956* London: Methuen

Brosh, H (1996) Arabic to Hebrew Speakers in Israel – 'Second Language' or 'Foreign Language' (published in Hebrew) *Helkat Lashon* 23, pp 111-131

Bronfenbrenner, U (1976) The Experimental Ecology of Education *Educational Researcher*, 5 pp 5-15

175

Bruner, JS (1986) *Actual Minds, Possible Worlds* Cambridge, Massachusetts: Harvard University Press

Cameron, D, Frazer, E, Harvey, P, Rampton, MBH and Richardson, K (1992) *Researching Language: Issues of Power and Method* London: Routledge

Cazden, C (1988) *Classroom Discourse: The Language of Teaching and Learning* Portsmouth, NH: Heinemann

Clandenin, DJ and Connelly, FM (1994) Personal Experience Methods in: Denzin, NK and Lincoln, Y (eds) *Handbook of Qualitative Research* Thousand Oaks, California: Sage

Clandenin, D J and Connelly, FM (2000) *Narrative Enquiry: Experience and Story in Qualitative Research* San Francisco: Jossey-Bass

Clifford, J (1988) *The Predicament of Culture: Twentieth-Century Ethnography, Literature, and Art* Cambridge, Massachusetts and London, England: Harvard University Press

Clifford, J (1997) *Routes: Travel and Translation in the Late Twentieth Century* Cambridge, Massachusetts and London, England: Harvard University Press

Cole, M (1985) The Zone of Proximal Development: where Culture and Cognition Create Each Other in: Wertsch, JV (ed) *Culture, Communication and Cognition: Vygotskyan Perspectives* New York: Cambridge University Press pp 146-161

Cole, M (1996) *Cultural Psychology: a Once and Future Discipline* Cambridge, Massachusetts and London, England: The Belknap Press of Harvard University Press

Comte, A (1973) *Systems of Positive Policy* (Revised ed) New York: B Franklin (originally published in 1875)

Conteh, J (1990) Children Reading Behind the Lines, *Multicultural Teaching*, 8(2) pp 34-38

Conteh, J (2000) Multilingual Classrooms, Standards and Quality: Three Children and a Lot of Bouncing Balls *Language and Education*, 14(1) pp 1-17

Conteh, J (2003) *Succeeding in Diversity: Culture, Language and Learning in Primary Classrooms* Stoke-on-Trent: Trentham Books

Cook-Gumperz, J (1977) Situated Instructions: The Language Socialisation of School Age Children in: Ervin-Tripp, S and Mitchell-Kiernan, C (eds) *Child Discourse* NY: Academic Press pp 103-121

Cortazzi, M (1993) *Narrative Analysis* London: Falmer Press

Coulon, A (1995) *Ethnomethodology* Thousand Oaks, California: Sage

Cummins, J (1984) *Bilingualism and Special Education: Issues in Assessment and Pedagogy* Clevedon: Multilingual Matters

deCastell, S and Walker, T (1991) Identity, Metamorphosis and Ethnographic Research: What Kind of Story is 'Ways with Words'? *Anthropology and Education Quarterly*, 22(1) pp 3-20

Delpit, LD (1995) I Just Want to be Myself: Discovering What Students Bring to School 'In their Blood' in: Ayers, W (ed) *To Become a Teacher: Making a Difference in Children's Lives* New York: Teachers College Press, pp 34-48

Denzin, NK (1997) *Interpretive Ethnography: Ethnographic Practices for the 21st Century* Thousand Oaks, California: Sage

Drew, P (1990) Conversation Analysis (entry in: *Encyclopaedia of Language and Linguistics*, Pergamon)

Durkheim, E (1956) *Education and Sociology* Glencoe, Il: The Free Press

Edwards, D and Mercer, N (1987) *Common Knowledge: the Development of Understanding in the Classroom* London: Methuen

Ely, M, Vinz, R, Downing, M and Anzul, M (1997) *On Writing Qualitative Research: Living by Words* London: Falmer

Fairclough, N (1989) *Language and Power* London: Longman

Ferguson, CA (1959) Diglossia *Word*, 15, pp 325-40

Fivush, R and Neisser, U (1996) *The Remembered Self* New York: Cambridge University Press

Flick, U (1998) *An Introduction to Qualitative Research* London: Sage

Francis, H (1993) Advancing Phenomenography: Questions of Method *Nordisk Pedagogik*, 2 pp 68-75

Freeman, M (1993) *Rewriting the Self: History, Memory, Narrative* London and New York: Routledge

Fyle, CN and Jones, ED (1980) *A Krio-English Dictionary* Oxford: Oxford University Press

Garfinkel, H (1967) *Studies in Ethnomethodology* New-Jersey: Prentice-Hall, Inc

Gee, J P (1989) Literacy, Discourse and Linguistics: Essays by James Paul Gee *Journal of Education*, 17(1)

Gee, JP (1991) A Linguistic Approach to Narrative, *Journal of Narrative and Life History*, 1 pp 15-40

Gee, JP (1992) *The Social Mind: Language, Ideology and Social Practice* New York: Series in Language and Ideology, Macedo, D (ed) Bergin and Garvey

Gee, JP (1996) *Social Linguistics and Literacies* London: Falmer Press

Geertz, C (1973) *The Interpretation of Cultures* New York: Basic Books

Geertz, C (1983) *Local Knowledge* New York: Basic Books

Geertz, C (1988) *Works and Lives: The Anthropologist as Author* Cambridge: Polity Press

Geertz, C (1995) *After the Fact, Two Countries, Four Decades, One Anthropologist* Cambridge, Massachusetts: Harvard University Press

Geertz, C (2000) *Available Light: Reflections on Philosophical Topics* Princeton, NJ and Oxford: Princeton University Press

Gellner, E (1998) *Language and Solitude* Cambridge: Cambridge University Press

Gergen, KJ (1989) Warranting Voice and the Elaboration of Self in: Shotter, J and Gergen, KJ, (eds) *Texts of Identity* London: Sage

Gergen, KJ (1994) *Realities and Relationships* Cambridge Massachusetts: Harvard University Press

Gergen, M (1992) Life Stories: Pieces of a Dream in: Rosenwald, GC and Ochberg RL (eds) *Storied Lives: The Cultural Politics of Self Understanding* Yale University Press

Gilroy, P (1992) Ethnic Absolutism in: Grossman, N and Treichler, PA (eds) *Cultural Studies* New York: Routledge

Giroux, H (1991) *Border Crossings* London: Routledge

Gitlin, A, Siegel, M and Boru, K (1989) The Politics of Method: from Leftist Ethnography to Educative Research, *Qualitative Studies in Education*, 2(3) pp 237-253

Glaser, BG and Strauss, AL (1967) *The Discovery of Grounded Theory* Chicago: Aldine

Goodman, YM (1990) Discovering Children's Inventions of Writing Language in: Goodman, YM (ed) *How Children Contrast Literacy* Newark, Delaware: IRA, pp 1-11

Gregory, E (1990) Negotiation as a Criterial Factor in Learning to Read in a Second Language *Language and Education*, 4(2) pp 103-115

Gregory, E (1993) What Counts as Reading in the Early Years Classroom? *British Journal of Educational Psychology*, 63(2) pp 214-230

Gregory, E (1994-6) *Family Literacy History and Children's Learning at Home and at School*, (with Jane Mace) ESRC: R-0000-22-1186

Gregory, E (1996) *Making Sense of a New World: Learning to Read in a Second Language* London: Paul Chapman

Gregory, E (1999-2000) *Siblings as Mediators of Literacy in Two East London Communities*, ESRC: R-000-22-2487

Gregory, E and Williams, A (2000) *City Literacies: Learning to Read Across Generations and Cultures*, London: Routledge

Gregory, E (2003-4) *Intergenerational Learning Between Grandparents and Young Children in East London*, (with C Kenner and J Jessel) ESRC: RES-000-22-0131

Halliday, MAK (1973) Relevant Models of Language in: Halliday, MAK *Explorations in the Functions of Language* London: Edward Arnold pp 9-21

Hammersley, M and Atkinson P (1997, 2nd ed) *Ethnography* New York: Routledge

Harvey, D (1989) *The Condition of Postmodernity* London: Blackwell

Hatch, JA and Wisniewski, R (1995) *Life History and Narrative* London: Falmer Press

Heap, JL (1985) Discourse in the Production of Classroom Knowledge: Reading Lessons *Curriculum Inquiry*, 16(1) pp 245-279

Heath, S Brice (1982a) Ethnography in Education: Defining the Essentials in: Gilmore, P and Glatthorn, AA (eds) *Children In and Out of School: Ethnography and Education Washington*, DC: Center for Applied Linguistics pp 33-58

Heath, S Brice (1982b) Questioning at Home and at School: A Comparative Study in: Hammersley, M (ed) *Case Studies in Classroom Research* Philadelphia: Open University Press pp 104-132

Heath, S Brice (1982c) What No Bedtime Story Means: Narrative Skills at Home and School *Language in Society*, 2(2) pp 49-76

Heath, S Brice (1983) *Ways with Words: Life and Work in Communities and Classrooms* Cambridge: Cambridge University Press

Heath, S Brice (1993) The Madness(es) of Reading and Writing Ethnography, *Anthropology and Education Quarterly*, 24(3) pp 256-268

Heritage, J (1984) *Garfinkel and Ethnomethodology* Cambridge: Polity Press

Hilbert, RA (1993) *The Classical Roots of Ethnomethodology* Chapel Hill: University of North Carolina Press

Hymes, DH (1973) On the Origins and Foundations of Inequality among Speakers in: Haugen, E and Bloomfield, M (eds) *Language as a Human Problem* New York: WW Norton and Co

Hymes, DH (1981) Ethnographic Monitoring in: Trueba, HT, Guthrie, GP and Au, KH (eds) *Culture and the Bilingual Classroom: Studies in Classroom Ethnography* Rowley, Massachusetts: Newbury House pp 56-68

Hymes, DH (1996) *Ethnography, Linguistics, Narrative Inequality: Towards an Understanding of Voice* London: Taylor and Francis

Innes, G (1969) *A Mende-English Dictionary* Cambridge: Cambridge University Press

Iser, W (1974) *The Implied Reader* Baltimore and London: The John Hopkins University Press

Jordan, S and Yeomans, D (1995) Critical Ethnography: Problems in Contemporary Theory and Practice, *British Journal of Sociology of Education*,16(3) pp 389-408

Kamil, ML, Langer, JA and Shanahan, T (1985) *Understanding Research in Reading and Writing* New York: Alleyn and Bacon

Kearney, C (1990) Open Windows *English in Education*, 24(3) pp 3-13

Kearney, C (1998a) Deep Excavations: an Examination of the Tangled Roots of Identity in Modern Cosmopolitan Societies *International Journal of Inclusive Education*, 2(4) pp 309-26

Kearney, C (1998b) Whose Future is it Anyway?: the National Curriculum and the Next Century *Goldsmiths Journal of Education* 1(2) pp 2-14

Kearney, C (2000) Eyes Wide Shut: Recent Educational Policy in the Light of Changing Notions of English Identity *English in Education*, 34(3) pp 19-30

Kelly, G (1955) *A Theory of Personality* Mass: The Norton Library

Kerlinger, FN (1972) *Foundations of Behavioural Research* New York: Holt, Rinehart and Winston

Labov, W (1972a) *Language in the Inner-City: Studies in Black English Vernacular* Oxford: Basil Blackwell

Labov, W (1972b) *Sociolinguistic Patterns* Philadelphia, PA: University of Pennsylvania

Langer, S (1941) *Philosophy in a New Key: a Study in the Symbolism of Reason, Rite and Art* Cambridge, Massachusetts and London, England: Harvard University Press

Lavie, S and Swedenburg T (1996) *Displacement, Diaspora and Geographies of Identity* Durham and London: Duke University Press

Lincoln, YS and Guba, EG (1985) *Naturalistic Enquiry* Thousand Oaks, California: Sage

Malinowski, B (1922) *The Argonauts of the Western Pacific* London: Routledge and Kegan Paul

McDermott, RP and Roth, DR (1978) The Social Organization of Behaviour: Interactional Approaches *Annual Review of Anthropology*, 7 pp 321-345

McDermott, RP and Tylbour, H (1983) On the Necessity of Collusion *Text*, 3(3) pp 277-297

Meek, M (1988/1997) *How Texts Teach What Readers Learn* Avonset, UK: Thimble Press

Meek, M (1991) *On Being Literate* London: The Bodley Head/Random House

Mehan, H (1981) Ethnography of Bilingual Education in: Trueba, HT, Guthrie, GP and Au, KH (eds) *Culture and the Bilingual Classroom: Studies in Classroom Ethnography* Rowley, Massachusetts: Newbury House, pp 36-55

Michaels, S (1986) Narrative Presentations: an Oral Preparation for Literacy with First Graders in: Cook-Gumperz, J (ed) *The Social Construction of Literacy* Cambridge: Cambridge University Press, pp 94-116

Mishler, EG (1990) Validation in Inquiry-guided Research: the Role of Exemplars in Narrative Studies *Harvard Educational Review*, 60(4) pp 415-442

Mor, A (1997) A Journey into a New Language: Literacy in Second Language – a Case Study (published in Hebrew) in: Eshel, M (ed) *Literacy: Theory and Practice*, No 4 Haifa: Gordon Teachers College pp 11-27

Mor-Sommerfeld, A (2002) Language Mosaic. Developing Literacy in a Second-New Language: a New Perspective *Reading Literacy and Language*, 36(3) pp 99-106

Morson, GS and Emerson, C (1990) *Mikhail Bakhtin: Creation of a Prosaics* California: Stanford University Press

Neill, AS (1968) *Summerhill* Harmondsworth: Penguin

Ochs, E (1979) Transcription as Theory in: Ochs, E and Schieffelin, BB *Developmental Pragmatics* New York: Academic Press, Inc, pp 43-72

Ogbu, JU (1981) School Ethnography: a Multilevel Approach *Anthropology and Education Quarterly*, 12(1) pp 3-29

Peshkin, A (1988) In Search of Subjectivity – One's Own *Educational Researcher*, Oct, pp17-22

Philips, S (1972) Participant Structures and Communicative Competence: Warm Springs Children in Community and Classroom in: Cazden, C, Hymes, D and John, VJ (eds) *Functions of Language in the Classroom* New York: Teachers College Press, pp 370-394

Polyani, M (1958) *Personal Knowledge* Chicago, Ill: University of Chicago Press

Pring, R (1976) *Knowledge and Schooling* London: Open Books

Rajchman, J (1995) *The Identity in Question* New York: Routledge

Randall, WL (1995) *The Stories We Are: An Essay on Self Creation* Toronto: University of Toronto Press

Reissman, CK (1993) *Narrative Analysis* Thousand Oaks California: Sage

Rigg, P, and Allen, VG (1989) *When They Don't All Speak English* Urbana, Illinois: National Council of Teachers of English

Rist, RC (1970) Student Social Class and Teacher Expectations: the Self-fulfilling Prophecy in the Ghetto *Harvard Educational Review*, 40(3) pp 411-451

Rosenwald, GC and Ochberg RL (eds) (1992) *Storied Lives: The Cultural Politics of Self Understanding* Yale University Press

Said, Edward (1987) *Orientalism* London: Routledge

Santa Barbara Discourse Group (1992a) Do you See What We See? the Referential and Intertextual Nature of Classroom Life *Journal of Classroom Interaction*, 27(2) pp 29-36

Santa Barbara Discourse Group (1992b) Constructing Literacy in Classrooms: Literate Action as Social Accomplishment in: Marshall, HH (ed) *Redefining Student Learning: Roots of Educational Change* Norwood, NJ: Ablex pp 119-150

Santa Barbara Discourse Group (1995) Constructing an Integrated, Inquiry-oriented Approach in Classrooms: a Cross-case Study of Social, Literate and Academic Practices *Journal of Classroom Interaction*, 30(2) pp 1-15

Sarbin, TR and Scheibe, KE (eds) (1983) *Studies in Social Identity* New York: Praeger Publishers

Schieffelin, BB and Cochran-Smith, M (1984) Learning to Read Culturally: Literacy before Schooling in: Goelman, H, Oberg, A and Smith, F (eds) *Awakening to Literacy* Victoria: Heinemann Educational

Schutz, A (1962) *Collected Papers (I): The Problem of Social Reality* The Hague: Martinus Nijhoff

Silverman, D (1993) *Interpreting Qualitative Data* London: Sage

Simpson, J (1992, July 18) The Closing of the American Media *The Spectator,* p9

Smith, F (1983) Reading Like a Writer *Language Arts* 60 pp 558-567

Smith, F (1988) *Understanding Reading: A Psycholinguistic Analysis of Reading and Learning to Read* Hillsdale, New Jersey: Erlbaum

Smith, F (1992) *To Think in Language, Learning and Education* London: Routledge

Spengmann, WC (1980) *The Forms of Autobiography: Episodes in the History of a Literary Genre* New Haven, Conn: Yale University Press

Tierney, WG and Lincoln, YS (eds) (1997) *Representation and the Text: Re-Framing the Narrative Voice* New York: State University of New York Press

Trueba, HT (1989) *Raising Silent Voices: Educating the Linguistic Minorities for the Twenty-first Century* Rowley, Massachusetts: Newbury House

Tunley, P, Travers, T and Pratt, J (1979) *Depriving the Deprived* London: Kogan Page

Van Maanen, J (1988) *Tales from the Field: On Writing Ethnography* Chicago: University of Chicago Press

Varenne, H and McDermott, R (1998) *Successful Failure: The Schools America Builds* Colorado: Westview Press

Vygotsky, L (1978) *Mind in Society* Cambridge, Mass: Harvard University Press

Vygotsky, LS (1986) *Thought and Language* Cambridge, Mass: The MIT Press

Watson-Gegeo, KA (1988) Ethnography in ESL: Defining the Essentials *TESOL Quarterly,* 22(4), pp 575-592

Wells, G (1986) *The Meaning Makers* London: Hodder and Stoughton

Willes, MJ (1983) *Children into Pupils* London: Routledge

Wolcott, H (1975) Criteria for an Ethnographic Research in Schools, *Human Organisation,* 34(2) pp 111-127

Woods, P (1996) *Researching the Art of Teaching: Ethnography for Educational Use* London: Routledge

Index